Also by Ann Weiler Walka: *Waterlines: Journeys on a Desert River*

# Walking The Unknown River
## and Other Travels
## in Escalante Country

# Walking The Unknown River
## and Other Travels
## in Escalante Country

Ann Weiler Walka

In cooperation with the
Museum of Northern Arizona

Flagstaff, Arizona
and
Bluff, Utah

Book designed and illustrated by Mary Williams
Cover photograph by Norm Shrewsbury

Copyright © 2002 by Ann Weiler Walka

Published by Bluff City Books
Flagstaff, Arizona
and
Bluff, Utah

Distributed by Vishnu Temple Press
P.O. Box 30821
Flagstaff, Arizona 86003-0821
928-556-0742
info@vishnutemplepress.com

ISBN 0-9718892-0-1

## Dedication

To Joe,
and home.

## Acknowledgements

MY THANKS to the Museum of Northern Arizona, Four Corners School, and Canyonlands Field Institute, remarkable institutions which practice and model devotion to place, for sending me on most of the journeys I write about here. And to Don Keller, my long-time hiking partner, for both his field sense and his far-ranging imagination. And, of course, to all the travelers who have scrambled over this stony landscape with me. I have learned much from all of you.

"The Unknown River," the poem, first appeared in *Testimony: Writers of the West Speak on Behalf of Utah Wilderness*, edited by Stephen Trimble and Terry Tempest Williams and published in 1996 by Milkweed Editions. "Climbing at Night at Scorpion Butte" was published in *Borderlands: Texas Poetry Review*. "Dance Hall Rock" and "Flow Report" appeared in *The Canyon Echo*. "Inquiries for Amphibians" appeared in *City Arts*. Parts of the "The River Flowing" and "Surveying the Outback" appeared in "Glen Canyon: A Canyon Transformed," *Plateau* 65:2, 1994 (Museum of Northern Arizona).

# Contents

River Notes ....... 1
Introduction ....... 3
*Reading the Map* ....... 8

## The Unknown River
*Off Forty-Mile Ridge* ....... 12
Walking the Escalante ....... 13
Mapping the Plateau ....... 16
*The Unknown River* ....... 18
Rocks ....... 19
*A Geologic History* ....... 21
*Exotica* ....... 22
*Lost in Space* ....... 23
Rain ....... 24
*Desert Erotica* ....... 26
*Inquiries for Amphibians* ....... 27
A River Flowing ....... 28

## Glen Canyon of the Colorado
Glen Canyon of the Colorado ....... 32
*The Glen* ....... 35
*Glen Canyon: A Species List* ....... 36
*Wild Heart* ....... 37
Un-naming the Country ....... 38
*A Lament* ....... 41
The Reservoir ....... 42
*The New Lake* ....... 45
*The Unhaunting* ....... 46
*The Heart of the Matter* ....... 47
Letting Go the River ....... 48
*Cycles* ....... 52
Another Glen ....... 53

## Navajo Mountain

| | |
|---|---|
| Natsis' áán | 58 |
| *Topography* | 62 |
| Patterns | 63 |
| *Circles* | 65 |
| Surveying the Outback | 66 |
| *Making a Home* | 69 |
| Tracks | 70 |
| Sleeping Out | 73 |
| *Sleeping on the Lap of Earth Woman* | 75 |
| *Lullaby* | 76 |

## Coming Home

| | |
|---|---|
| Dance Hall Rock | 80 |
| *Dance Hall Rock* | 82 |
| Into the Canyon | 84 |
| *Climbing at Night at Scorpion Butte* | 87 |
| *Local Knowledge* | 88 |
| Harris Wash | 90 |
| *Finding the Patterns: The Poet as Scientist* | 92 |
| *The Mayfly* | 94 |
| Coming Home | 95 |
| *Flow Report* | 98 |

| | |
|---|---|
| Sources of Quotations | 101 |
| References | 102 |

Walking The Unknown River

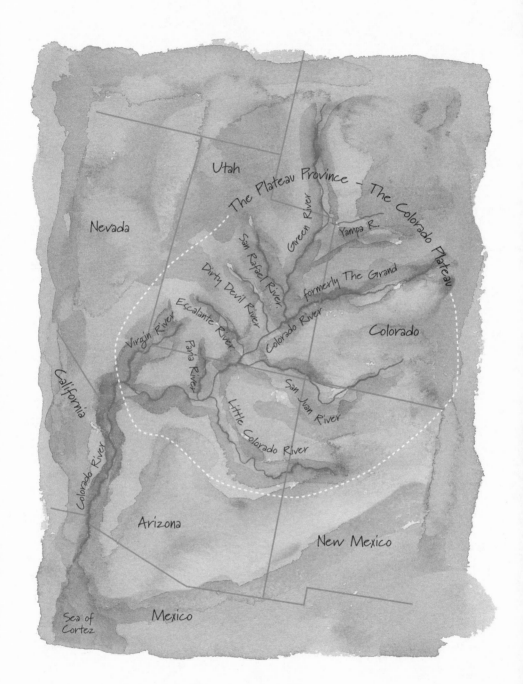

The Great River

# River Notes

WHY DO WE IMAGINE rivers as sinuous lines bisecting landscapes? They are far more complicated in form, as intricately branched as any wind-gnarled spruce at timberline. Rivulets form at the melting edges of snowbanks, or on a rainwashed slickrock face, and are drawn together by gravity as surely as by fate. Streamlets pair and pair again, ephemeral flows pouring into perennial streams, and perennial streams—rivers themselves, perhaps—by now converging into a twisted, branched mainstem, the waters of a basin going down to the sea.

In this way the Colorado River system drains 140,000 square miles of the elevated, iron-stained Plateau Province. The great river comprises a dendritic arrangement of rills and rivulets and creeks and streams gathered into a mainstream which flows off to the Pacific at the Sea of Cortez. Connected in one of nature's most basic patterns, this "tree" of tributaries is all one river. Ah, but humans separate and name. And rename.

The Colorado's two major branches converge above Glen Canyon. On John Wesley Powell's maps, the longer tributary, which forms in the Wind River Mountains in Wyoming, was named the Green after the more musical Rio Verde. The other fork, heading in the Never Summer range of Colorado's Rocky Mountains, was labeled the Grand River. Deep in the canyon country, where the Green and Grand joined, the mighty Colorado came into its own identity.

These names overlay earlier generations of Native American and Spanish names, and are ephemeral themselves. In the 1920s, the Colorado state legislature renamed the Grand after their state. With this name change came a perceptual one. Although earlier travelers recognized the longer, more intricately branched Green as the main fork of the Colorado River, the headwaters are now popularly imagined to rise in the Colorado Rockies.

In the reach of water Powell named Glen Canyon, the great river is fattened by the Dirty Devil, Escalante, San Juan, and Paria Rivers, and by countless seasonal streams. No matter these separate names, the family tree is Colorado.

Glen Canyon Outback

# Introduction

*It is through the power of observation, the gifts of eye and ear, of tongue and nose and finger, that a place first rises up in our mind; afterwards it is memory that carries the place, that allows it to grow in depth and complexity. For as long as our records go back, we have held these two things dear, landscape and memory. Each infuses us with a different kind of life.*

Barry Lopez

THE BLUE LACCOLITHIC DOME Anglos named Navajo Mountain beckons like a lodestone above the Glen Canyon basin. From a distance the silhouette, both massive and as airy as rain, might be a river cobble perched on the straight edged, iron-stained mesas, or the dream of a cobble. Navajos know this dome as the head of Earth Woman, a powerful being who reclines across the Four Corners region.

They say two sacred rivers made love at her base, the steeper-pitched San Juan covering the mainstream, the Colorado, their union conceiving the rain. The waters of another little river, the Escalante, flowed into the Colorado a few miles upstream. These three rivers joined at the heart of Glen Canyon which was, in turn, the heart of the high, dry, lonesome physiographic province called the Colorado Plateau. The confluences are silenced now by Lake Powell, but Earth Woman still overlooks the reservoir.

Once wilderness stretched off from Navajo Mountain in every direction, sandstone fretted into canyons and pushed up in folds and mesas. Here streams that sculpt the Glen Canyon basin, the catchment area for the stretch of the Colorado from the mouth of the Dirty Devil to the mouth of the Paria, drain the rain and snowmelt from a vast sweep of country. Water gathers from the Kaiparowits and Aquarius Plateaus, the Circle Cliffs, Waterpocket Fold, and the Henrys, as well as Navajo Mountain and her rainbow mesas. For millions of years, these creeks, pairing and pairing again, flowed beneath Earth Woman's gaze toward Grand Canyon.

And for millennia local folk crisscrossed the quiet, more accessible stretches of the Colorado, the San Juan and the Escalante. Before the Navajo arrived, the Paiute and their Ute cousins passed lightly through this "land of frozen rainbows," harvesting the meager bounty of the high desert. Earlier yet the Colorado made a frontier, albeit a permeable one, between backwoods Puebloan farmers and their northern Fremont neighbors. In deeper time, a charred bone, a pinch of seed were left here and there by Archaic hunters and gatherers.

Two hundred years ago, the first Europeans came on horseback to the foot of Glen Canyon. In the year the Declaration of Independence was signed, an apparently reluctant God revealed a river crossing to Fathers Dominguez and Escalante as a way back home to Santa Fe.

In the 1850s Mormon farmers settled the arable margins of the basin. The Navajo and the Mormons used the handful of familiar fords; the Navajo to hunt and to raid the Mormons and the Mormons first to proselytize the Indians and then, improbably enough, for wagon crossings.

Lightly inhabited and scarcely charted, the region beckoned nineteenth-century explorers as an empty space on the American maps. After the Civil War, John Wesley Powell arrived at Glen Canyon by boat and set off an era of adventure and exploration. His first descent of the Colorado River and the resulting government-backed survey, brought the Great Unknown into the annals of science and finance. Robert Stanton surveyed a railroad route through the Colorado's canyons from Green River, Utah, to the Gulf of Mexico before he came back to the Glen with a gold dredge named the Hoskannini. Two brothers from Grand Canyon, Ellsworth and Emery Kolb, first rowed down from Wyoming on the adventure of a lifetime and then returned to help with dam site surveys. Prospectors dragged wooden scows up the Colorado and the San Juan and floated down looking for gold in the river silts.

Halfway through the twentieth century, Earth Woman's purview remained obscure if fabled country. Despite the abundance of foot trails, the rocky terrain was difficult for horses and murder for wheels. There were no paved roads and no bridges across the Colorado from Moab to Lees Ferry, nearly three hundred miles, until the late 1950s. Nor for a hundred and forty miles up the San Juan, where the bridge at Mexican Hat was so shaky that uranium haulers had to dump half their load before they crossed. Nor past countless bends of the Escalante to the mouth of Calf Creek. Every crossing, every river trip, was a singular accomplishment.

IN 1963 THE Glen Canyon Dam, fifty-some miles downstream from Navajo Mountain, stopped the Colorado, the Escalante and the San Juan Rivers in their tracks. Over the next twenty years, the still waters of Lake Powell inundated 150 miles, virtually all of Glen Canyon of the Colorado. The reservoir's arms forked twenty-seven miles up the Escalante and seventy miles up the San Juan.

Crossings are humdrum now; paved highways come down to the water and two new bridges span Glen Canyon. Two million tourists arrive every year to marvel at and play on a startling blue lake with a barren, crooked coastline longer than California's. Make no mistake, marvels still abound in the greater, largely untouched, Glen Canyon drainage. The upper Escalante runs free, winding through a deep canyon draining the Aquarius Plateau. Dubbed the "Unknown River" by John Wesley Powell's cartographer, the Escalante was the last river in the lower forty-eight to be mapped. Above the streambed, the sandstones of the Glen Canyon group recall the Eden drowned downstream.

And up on the rims, away from the farflung highways and the marinas and airstrips, a maze of rock is still the back of the beyond. The High Plateaus, the Kaiparowits, and Waterpocket Fold stand inscrutable beyond the canyons of the Escalante. Across the Colorado, Navajo Mountain rises above a separate nation.

Despite the communications towers on the crown of her head, Earth Woman gazes benevolently over the mesatops. Hiking around the mountain, one walks into another time. You can still get lost for a while, or die of thirst. The heroes of creation stories seem far more present than any twentieth-century icons. The lake when it catches your eye from some high butte is simply an illusion.

Most visitors now know the Glen Canyon basin as the Lake and the edge of the Lake, a stark and stunning landscape. They seldom venture into the difficult terrain beyond the edge, terrain overlain with human hubris and travail, with stories and ceremony. The country remains as mysterious as an omnipotent mind. A lifetime of exploring Glen Canyon's basin, in real time and in memory, would not decipher it all.

MY OWN TRAVELS HERE have been largely as a guide and a naturalist, either scouting trips or bringing groups into the country. I aim to tutor my guests in the practice of learning—and of fitting into—a place. I dream that the compelling, unfamiliar scenery may awaken in them a naturalist's mindfulness and passion to belong that will reach all the way home. Mostly immigrants, we need a way, in Kim Stafford's words, to achieve a "rooted companionship" with our chosen ground on this adopted continent.

Learning a place is not a linear project. On these ventures we start with Lopez's "power of observation, the gifts of eye and ear, of tongue and nose and finger." Resting from sensory intoxication, we hear local stories and first-hand accounts of other explorations here. With our bundle of field guides and our collective great brain, we try to identify the plants and animals and rock formations, and the connections among them, which keep Earth Woman's community humming along. We read poems and sometimes write them. We sit in silence. Day after day as we open to the country it opens to us.

As we poke about in Earth Woman's neighborhood, we acquire habits and tools for learning our own neighborhoods better. And remembering, we carry this far country back to our everyday habitats; not just its colors and its quiet, its scenic wonders, but its wisdom too. Journeying in wild places informs us about playfulness and responsibility, the solace of solitude and the comfort of belonging, the attractions of both coherence and uncertainty. On every trip I learn something new about right relationship or right livelihood.

IN THE SPIRIT OF my guiding here, this writing comprises a collectively remembered landscape. Like the assembled reports of any exploring expedition, like the place, it's layered here, enigmatic there, and far from linear. The stories are in many voices; two of my own—the naturalist and the poet—as well as those of explorers, pioneers, and a people whose oral traditions evoke the country's origins. I invite you to meander through this written landscape as you might any new terrain; follow a false trail, get lost or rimmed out, naturalize, daydream, circle back, penetrate further. Make yourself at home.

*It is a sublime panorama. The heart of the inner Plateau Country is spread out before us in a birds-eye view. It is a maze of cliffs and terraces lined off with stratification, of crumbling buttes, red and white domes, rock platforms gashed with profound canyons, burning plains barren even of sage all glowing with bright color and flooded with blazing sunlight. Nature has here made a geological map of the country and colored it so that we may read and copy it miles away.*

Clarence Dutton

# Reading the Map

In her hand a carefully folded map, a pencil line
lightly drawn down the inverted Vs
of drainages, around the concentric circles
of slickrock domes.

At her feet a maze of sandstone spalling off
from the red dirt road;  pink swells,
curious twists of shadow, patinated
walls that sheer into canyons
like sheets of rain.

They should match. She labors with her compass,
puzzling over the unfathomable angle
separating the north she has always
believed in, a red arrow pointing
straight and steady year after year,
from the mysterious True North.

Rotating the creased paper,
peering into the crumpled landscape,
she bends canyons with her mind,
like spoons, to fit them onto the elegantly
drawn map. The charted truths are inscrutable,
immutable data from another kingdom.

Shrugging her thin brown shoulders into her pack,
she grins at the notion of two landscapes,
each an enigma, and walks down the first wash
she encounters.

Mapped, this stone lip where the stream hurtles
straight down when it rains
would be a cluster of lines
darkened into a single stroke of shadow.

On the map she would know
where she can scramble
up the broken spine of a ridge
and down into the next drainage.
Whether that canyon will drop off too.
She retraces her steps looking hard for the link
between landscape and construct.

Between perfect unreason;
rainstorms scoring naked rock like emery paper,
sweeping skiffs of dirt into streams
that carve and abrade and polish
with no plan at all, tumbling
under the sway of gravity
down the way of least resistance;

and perfect reason; country
sighted and measured, each detail
checked against the next, calibrated
to scale, meticulously plotted,
faithfully copied.

A dazzle of intuition,
and the two terrains resonate
under her felt hat. The map and the country
lead her down the only nose of rock
sloping gently enough for a cautious butt slide.
Onto a dune that pours into a finger
of canyon too choked with willow
to walk a backpack through
except by turning, ducking, bending branches.

She thrashes forward, head down,
shoulders parting waxen, pungent stems,
feeling her way to the river.

Hiking into Fox Canyon

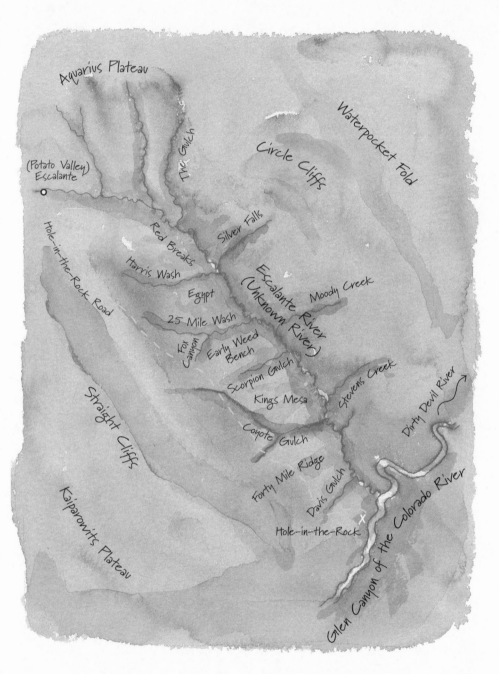

Canyons of the Escalante River

# The Unknown River

# Off Forty-Mile Ridge

she slipped through a crevice
too skinny for her pack, walking
off from home
and her mud-stippled truck,
and a low-screaming jet
that scared her belly-down
on red dirt.

Raised east of here
on a bluff above the Wabash,
spring always called her
back to a river.

Sliding down a dune
lit with green stripe lilies
and prickly phlox
she dropped her boots
in a dapple of new-
leafed cottonwoods.

Waded a creek
toward the Unknown River,
so-called by her people,
midwestern men,
hardpressed to imagine
that for generations
women gathered willow here
and tart red berries.

Splashed at last
into a clay-whitened stream
grinning at the water
coming down, coming down;
no beginning, no end;
parting around her,
hurrying on.

Coyote Gulch and the Escalante

# Walking the Escalante

IN EARLY APRIL night drowns the pale sand here
like chalky river water poured from a hiking boot.
A twig fire glowing on a battered cookie tin pulls
my companions shoulder to shoulder, fingers
stretched toward the hope of heat. At their backs
darkness wells from stone.

We forded the Escalante just at dusk, scratched
and crabby from thrashing our way down a side
canyon. Beavers, too prudent to build dams on the
river, assuaged their frustrations along the creek,
creating unwadable pools silted now and then into
thickets, excavating booby traps in the banks. And
above the beaver works, a pourover circumvented
by a climb, a scramble up a bald, slickrock shoulder
pitched too steep to stand upright on, and then a
sketchy route down.

Ordinarily agile, I stalled out halfway up the
slope, summiting shaky and embarrassed. Thinking
about it now while I work at a pot with a sliver of a
scrubby, I can feel my face flush against the wash of
cold air. What am I doing, running away from
home every few weeks, carrying everything including the kitchen sink on my back, aiding climbs I
barely make? This is the first day of my fifty-first
year. I feel like a tourist.

Chores done, I leave my new friends listening to
Don's guitar and use my foot to scoop a cradle in
sand sheltered by newly-leafed willows. Dry and
finally blessedly alone, I squirm into my sleeping
bag and let my spine relax at last. I prop my eyes
open, searching a curve of sky as starry as an
Appaloosa's rump, looking for my directions before
the moon rises. She passes over this break in the
sandstone sea without ever waking me.

SPRING AFTER SPRING I come back here to the
Escalante, the tributary flowing southeast into the
Colorado River from the Aquarius Plateau, halfway

down the now-dammed Glen Canyon. Sometimes
alone, often as a guide for the Museum of Northern
Arizona, I scramble down and up her side canyons
and over their divides, as well as walking the mainstream. This smaller river maintains the rhythms of
the once-mighty Colorado, flooding in the spring
freshet, a roaring slurry of mud after a summer
thunderbuster, lazy and low in the fall and winter.
A shapechanger, she undercuts the old terraces and
drops new ones, routs backwaters, abandons mean-
ders. Carved largely through a group of sandstones
named after Glen Canyon, the Escalante gorge is
laced with tributaries—Silver Falls, Scorpion
Gulch, Coyote—and spring-worn alcoves.

Major John Wesley Powell, the restless scientist
who first recorded this stretch of the Colorado
River country, preoccupied perhaps with some geological puzzle, floated past the mouth of the little
tributary without a second glance. Surveying by
land, Almon Thompson, Powell's brother-in-law,
added the "Unknown River" to the fast-growing
atlas of North America two years later.

A midwesterner like Powell and Thompson, I
often recount these two flatlanders' adventures to
my guests, my roots fingering deeper into sandrock
with each telling. While my own great-great-grand-
father went back to preaching the gospel according
to John Wesley after the Civil War, the Major led
two expeditions through the canyons of the Green
and the Colorado Rivers. These journeys, and
Thompson's reconnoiters on horseback, fixed much
of the Colorado River system on the new maps.
And Powell's accounts, rewoven into a captivating
yarn, introduced what Clarence Dutton, geologist,
called "innovations in scenery" to EuroAmericans.

Given the Major's omnivorous curiosity, it's odd
that no matter how distracting the geology, he
failed to notice the mouth of this little river. Lake

Powell now obscures the confluence, but in 1912 Ellsworth Kolb reported "a small muddy stream flowing from the north, in a narrow, rock-walled canyon." Perhaps the Major drifted by at low water, the old forest of willow and cottonwood along the Colorado's muddy bottom screening the tributary's lackadaisical flow.

AT FIRST LIGHT I pad in my stocking feet to the little arc of flat stones we call the kitchen, my running shoes still wet and gummed with river mud. By the time we finish coffee, sunshine spills over the sandstone wall and laps the gilia and lavender bushmint, the pale evening primroses flushed and wilting in the blossoming heat. The night forays of bugs and lizards and mice are impressed on the sand in a labyrinth of tracks that could take all morning to puzzle out. Perched on a willow, a Say's phoebe flicks her dark tail and calls, her *phew* a smooth pebble dropped into the limpid morning.

I love to walk. When I slip my arm through the strap of the pack balanced on my knee and do my little hop to swing it around and up, I grin to think of wading all day down the Unknown River. My body dragged in on its own, but in the night my heart caught up. I'm here now.

# Mapping the Plateau

THE AMERICAN PUBLIC, titillated by six months of rumored death and disaster, hailed Powell's first descent of the Colorado as a hero's tale. A second river exploration, this time with federal backing, was planned in two parts for the summers of 1871 and 1872. In the intervening winter Almon Thompson, along with his wife Ellen—Powell's botanizing sister—and her dog Fuzz, set up housekeeping in a cabin tent in Kanab, Utah. A school superintendant from Illinois, untrained in geology or geography, Thompson became the chief topographer of Powell's new Survey of the Colorado Country.

Riding out from base camp, Thompson undertook to triangulate the massive plateaus stepping up to the north and west of Glen Canyon, and to plot the maze of canyons which drained the high country into the Colorado. One of his major tasks was to solve the riddle of the Dirty Devil River.

Marking the head of Glen Canyon, the Dirty Devil flows into the Colorado to the east of the Henry Mountains, some miles upstream from the mouth of the Escalante. Having mapped the Dirty Devil on his first river trip in 1869, Powell chose its junction with the Colorado as a resupply point for the river trip of 1871. The Mormon packers, though, failed to find their way overland to the mouth of the "muddy, alkaline, undrinkable" stream.

Finding no provisions there, the hungry river crew cached an empty boat at the confluence of the Colorado and the Dirty Devil. They planned to send men by horseback the next spring to retrieve the boat and float on down to Kanab Creek where the other boats were waiting. Now the *Canonita* must be reclaimed.

FREDERICK DELLENBAUGH, a curious, sharp-eyed seventeen year-old who greatly admired "Prof," as the men called Thompson, for his "sunny way of looking on difficulties and obstacles as if they were mere problems in chess," recorded the mapping expeditions in his journal. A few days out of Kanab, Dellenbaugh reported that Thompson, last year's resupply chief Pardon Dodds, and the rest of the crew rode across Potato Valley, the grassy swale between the head of the Straight Cliffs and the Aquarius Plateau looming to the north. There, Dodds pointed out a stream which flowed off toward the canyons. Imagining this to be the Dirty Devil, he had ridden down it the summer before with his packstring, only to be thwarted by quicksand.

The party rode on, mounting ridge after ridge of vaulted sandstone "almost as steep as a horse can stand on." The men on foot heaved at their horses' flanks, urging them up steps hacked with axes.

Almon Thompson, a man not given to fretting about Utes or water or lost trails, eyed the sandstone maze like pieces of a jigsaw puzzle tossed out under a jay-blue sky. By eye he appraised the undulating strata and traced ridges and shadows, fitting them into the map forming in his head.

At night Thompson read aloud from Tennyson by a campfire sheltered in a stony ravine. Illinois farm boys, engulfed in an infernal knot of folds and canyons, warmed their chapped hands, leaning closer to the one bright fire anywhere.

Cresting the sandstones beyond Pardon Dodds' stream, the expedition picked its way across the "salient angle." The Henry Mountains, floated to the northeast rather than the west, across a "conglomeration of unknown mesas and canyons." Thompson saw that Dodds had followed the wrong river, a river the explorers had not yet noted.

He mapped this new tributary first as Potato Creek and then the Unknown River. Later he and Powell renamed it again for the good Father Escalante.

*The stream which we had followed and whose course soon became lost in the multitude of chasms before us was not the one we were in search of but an unknown, unnamed river, draining the eastern slope of the Aquarius Plateau and flowing through a deep, narrow canyon to the Colorado River. Believing our party to be the discoverers, we decided to call this stream in honor of Father Escalante, the old Spanish explorer.*

*Almon Thompson*

# The Unknown River

named finally on the American maps
after a Spaniard who never saw it but opened
a hundred years of Europeans in sandrock country.
A century of horses kicking stones down cliffs;
of hungry men huddled around the aromatic
heat of sagebrush fires; of curses
flung at sheer ridges and boulder-choked defiles.

The maps were drawn, revealing routes, obstacles, dead ends,
naming them, spelling out the country to the curious eyes
of politicans and prospectors, itinerant farmers
bent on water and a patch of soil.

                    Still, The Unknown
was not domesticated, being too sparse, too fierce
for more than a few hermits to settle,
no matter how many men appeared at the least rumor
of riches; digging up whole river banks; braving
quicksand for virgin grass.

                    Now hikers with fifty pound packs
scramble over boulders, ford a thigh-deep river
looking for miracles.

                  All this sweat notwithstanding,
the secrets hold. The shadows are not plumbed,
nor the springs traced to their cool hearts.

The Unknown is traveled but not penetrated,
studied but not deciphered,
mapped but not squared.

Egypt Bench

# Rocks

THIS SPRING—my forty-ninth—I'm a runaway, from teenage kids, museum education, being a dean's wife. Nearly new to this place but familiar too, I'm giddy with the fantasy of leaving the everyday forever and becoming a wild thing.  Each detail of my new habitat captivates me; the rock is spellbinding.

WALKING THE ESCALANTE toward its confluence with the Colorado, I'm enveloped by the stack of sedimentary strata that Thompson puzzled out on his way to the Dirty Devil. Powell and Thompson, raised like me in country deep with dirt and ruled off into fields, surely marvelled at all this bare rock too. At last night's camp, massive walls of Wingate sandstone curved around us, lightly chiseled with fans and arcs, whole sweeps varnished to blue-black or brushed with vertical strokes of burnt sienna. Now, down from the mouth of Moody Creek, the sheer base of the Wingate cliff juts from a Chinle talus slope high above the river. Sun-blasted slabs of sandstone, undercut as the shale erodes, litter the stream channel.

For tens of millions of arid years, sands were laid down on top of Triassic swamps by wind gusting from the northwest, and, during a wetter interlude, by streams winding across the desert. Buried, compacted, cemented, and finally folded up in a succession of Earthly shrugs, the Chinle swamps, Wingate dunes, ledgy Kayenta streambeds, and Navajo sandhills became the strata which form the canyons of the Escalante. (Eventually geologists collected the top three layers—Wingate, Kayenta and Navajo—into the Glen Canyon group.) Just yesterday in geologic time, these formations were cut through by the rivers.

The lithified dunes of the Navajo pillow the sky above my head. Their white domes evoke similes from my ordinarily literal, always ravenous

*July 29. The smooth, naked rock stretches out on either side of the river for many miles, but curiously carved mounds and cones are scattered everywhere and deep holes are worn out. Many of these pockets are filled with water.*

*July 30. Sometimes the canyon walls are vertical to the top; sometimes they are vertical below and have a mound covered slope above. We find that the orange sandstone is cut in two by a group of firm, calcareous strata, and the lower bed is underlain by soft, gypsiferous shales. One could almost imagine that the walls had been carved with a purpose, to represent giant architectural forms.*

*John Wesley Powell*

backpacking companions—dumplings, meringue, frozen custard. Powell originally named Glen Canyon for their rounded forms; Mound Canyon, from the Dirty Devil to the San Juan, and then Monument Canyon.

*Originally the surface of the Earth was a smooth plain, but one day Coyote told Hawk to place the latter's quiver at a short distance from where they stood that it might be used as a mark, at which he would shoot. Then Coyote sent an arrow from his bow which struck the quiver, but glanced and plowed its way about the face of the earth in every conceivable direction, digging deep gorges and canyons, making valleys, plowing up mountains, hills, and rocks.*

*A Paiute story recorded by John Wesley Powell*

OCCASIONALLY, SAND, weathered out of sandstone, reassembles in a living dune slanting up against a canyon wall. This evening, Don Keller, my backpacking colleague and a far better route-finder than I, leads our trudge up a sandhill to the rim of the side canyon while I stay behind to watch over the strays. Sometimes this sweeping business, being the tail instead of the brains of the line, brings out the bad kid in me. Today I delight in our journey up through the strata, our emergence from the tight, brushy canyon bottom toward the never-never of space and sky.

Bent under our loads, we plod like darkling beetles, two steps up and one back. Although our food is nearly gone after five days out, we're carrying enough water to dry camp up closer to the trailhead, full bottles on our backs, trading off two five-gallon jugs. Fortunately our eyes are downcast, and the lilies—wild onion and green stripe—thriving in the sand dune aquifer light our way.

At dusk we arrive in the terrain the Prof mused over as he tried to unravel the canyon system from above. As we thread our way among pale pockets of sand and just-opening evening primrose, stone dunes billow like clouds above our heads. A runaway could live forever here, if the mounds were really dumplings and the potholes deep enough.

Surely the Prof is still around, cross-legged on some dome, watching the day transmute from blue to lavender, a laconic, even-tempered plainsman sorting out the eons, placing the topography into a map forming in his mind.

# A Geologic History

Sand, swept along by a dark bird of a wind,
eddied into dunes. For years fledglings smoothed
and sculpted them, nudged them south

until grain by polished grain the hills
settled into inertia. Finally they were stilled
by water trickling through their limbs,

their restless hearts. Sand rustlings
gave way to the hum of bees trapped
when their burrows turned to stone.

Who knows when the cracks began to open;
hairline fractures widened
by a persistent root, a January freeze.

On summer afternoons lizards scratch
at the crevices, and molting snakes rub
out of their skins. The bees,

smelling resurrection, set to work
with their wings. The floods come down.
Tonight an oval moon, unveiled

after a sudden storm, illuminates
the intersection of two crevasses.
The poolful of tree frogs bawls with delight.


Beneath the Red Breaks

Exotica

A child of the Midwest
he must have pined
for exotica.

Medieval mosques
shining milk-white
under a three-quarter

moon; silver tusks
slicing the African night;
the Southern Cross.

Here, after mapping
all day, he waded
in moonlight that rolled

drop by drop down
sandstone scrolls,
billowed among

pillows of shadow
and silken seed,
lapped pebbles

into quicksilver.
Perfumes over-
flowed corollas

and brimmed
among gunmetal hills.
Toads shrilled

like stars. I wonder
was this far enough
to go clear?

Kings Mesa

## Lost in Space

At night the stone hills rise and fall,
folding over in steel-gray waves. Odd how
once we perceived them as landlocked,
mappable; now we must plot

our course by the heavens. We are lost,
three of us, feeling our way along
the crossbedding of an antiquarian storm,
distracted by sweet-smelling winds,

the dark gleam of a pool.
Twice we are pulled from landfall
by the moon's reflection. Celestial
navigation is an arcane art.

Disoriented by the ebb and swell, sky wheeling
overhead, we circle again, sleep-walking,
trying our best to believe at least
one star is fixed.


Scorpion Butte

# Rain

A FEW SPRINGS later it rains the whole week we're here. In fact, the clay road melts into tomato soup and we arrive a day late. The gentle river swells to a torrent of mud, hurling herself down to the Colorado. We can scarcely cross. Retreating up a mosquito-ridden ladder to higher country, we camp on a bench of Navajo sandstone, half-sheltered by pinyon pines.

We hunker here for three days, venturing out under the inky, fast-moving clouds to explore the desert awash, and retreating to high ground at night, anxious, always, to see if our tents survived. My mood veers from crankiness to elation at the aliveness of it all, water splashing over rock, sky rivers, the smell of pine and sage. The first night a squall howled in at dinner time, and Don and I struggled to tie down a tarp, snapping at each other, at the damned weather. We all crowded shoulder to shoulder under the leaky tarp for supper and stories, watching for the rare, otherworldly headlights on Boulder Mountain.

*After we had gone three leagues we were stopped for a long time by a strong blizzard and tempest consisting of rain and thick hailstones amid horrendous thunder claps and lightning flashes.*
*We recited the Virgin's Litany, for her to implore some relief for us, and God willed for the tempest to end.*

*Father Escalante*

I fell asleep to the thrum of rain, my hair damp, my clothes soggy and, thanks be to my paranoia, my sleeping bag dry. This weather and the attention required to keep folks comfortable has initiated me; neither feckless runaway nor tourist now, I'm a solid citizen of the sandrock country, making my guests at home. At first light, when I crawl out of my lavender tent into the clouds, the slickrock rustles and flows. A toad flounces across the glistening ledges. Water sheeting over stone funnels into streamlets, swirls down folds and pours over nickpoints, sweeps juniper dross and pine cones, sticks and seeds and sand toward the mainstream.

We're moved that way too. Threading a stone notch, we skirt close-packed gravels gleaming like burnished black pot sherds, trudge across flats stippled with yellow daisies and blue-eyed spider-wort, slide down a dune to the river bottom.

Sheltered in an alcove beside a mud-smoothed
Fremont granary, we watch the country transforming.
Waterfalls foam red into the already roaring little
river. Heavy with silt, the Escalante reworks her
bed, scouring the outside of the bends, moving
her sandbars downstream, reclaiming old second-
ary channels. New ground is being made here and
old ground giving way. After we go, tamarisk and
cottonwood will set seed on clean, new beaches.
Willows and cane grass may lose their footing, but
shoots will swell from the roots of the survivors.
Change is flagrant, unfettered, flush with promise.

*Happily, with abundant
dark clouds
may I walk.
Happily, with abundant
showers,
may I walk...
Happily may I walk.*

*The Night Chant,
The Ninth Day*

# Desert Erotica

For days we wandered over opulent stone
exploring shell pink vulvas, luminous
bellies tattooed with black lichen.

Beyond the river a cliff crested like
the inner curve of a thigh; gleaming
buttocks marked the way to camp.

Every evening, clouds crumpled
to blue violet and raveled into veils of
rain. We dreamed of freefalling

swirling in the helix of an ear,
the dimple of a navel.
                        Breaking camp
on a faintly shimmering, sage-struck

morning, we slipped single file
between ivory breasts. Emerged damp
and smooth-minded as seed.


Below the Red Breaks

# Inquiries for Amphibians

Bufo punctatus, red spotted toadlets,
popping from the shadow of my boot
like freckled jumping beans.

How is it, dear toadlets,
to slip from the embrace of water
and into the desert's spines and stones
drawn by an irresistible urge to burrow into sand
and grieve the silken days of childhood?

How is it to be born again into a shower of grace?


And you, Old Bufo Woodhousei, shaking off the ashes
of last night's fire.

How many winters have you hunkered in the dark
waiting for the fragrance of sage and mud
to lure you into an April rain?
Into a pool pulsing with the waaghs
and bleats of slick, satiny, belly-to-back love?

Is it fine, old Bufo, to be resurrected by holy rain
and rise directly into orgasm?


And little tree frog, Hyla reyna,
with your wasp waist, your thighs bulging
in their yellow tights, your forehead
begging to be kissed.

What about these seasons of bright blue,
golden-faceted days and long, deep sleeps,
light to dark, quick to still, and back again?

Do you dread the darkness and dream of light,
or is it the other way around?


Canyons of the Escalante

# A River Flowing

THE POINT at which Lake Powell silences the currents of the Unknown River changes as the water level in the reservoir rises and falls. I prefer to hike out of the Escalante's canyon before I meet that shifting, dispiriting edge. The bales of last year's tumbleweed and mats of driftwood piled up against the boulders at the flooded mouths of other tributaries are troubling enough. I like to remember the canyon of the Escalante as a vibrant world, enlivened by the rhythms of its river. Like Ed Abbey said, and an Irish poet before him, "I love all things that flow."

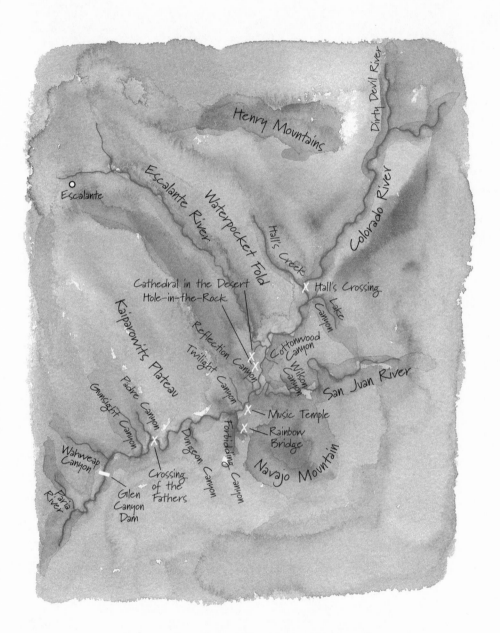

Glen Canyon of the Colorado

# Glen Canyon of the Colorado

SEVEN YEARS RUNNING I've cruised Lake Powell on the second week in October. I hardly ever confess this to my river friends who deplore lake boating as sacrilege.

On this autumn-lit afternoon, I'm chugging down the lake in a floating house trailer once again. Before it was damned, this reach of the Colorado River—from the mouth of the Dirty Devil up at Hite to the confluence with the Paria down at Lees Ferry—unfurled a skein of golden water from wall to sandstone wall through the old Glen Canyon. The river's glorious mud dropped out when the current stilled, and now the Colorado is a stalled-out, skinny strip of blue-black water hundreds of feet above the old streambed.

I'm driving—anyone can run a houseboat, but I'm skittish anyway—and reminiscing aloud about a Shangri-La I never saw. For me Glen Canyon is the stuff of dreams. As we hum between the rosy cliffs, I do my best to re-imagine for my guests the river beneath the main channel—a ferry at Halls Crossing, the Unknown River's secret entrance, summer quicksand.

We—I give up the pilot's seat for this move—park at the mouth of Wilson Canyon, just up the San Juan "arm" from the Glen itself. No matter how many river stories we spin to pass the time, our journey to the Rainbow Plateau at the foot of Navajo Mountain makes a long day of plowing flat-water.

A HALF HOUR LATER, I might be getting a whiff of the lost Eden. Shirking my cook's chores to recover from a day on the houseboat, I follow a ledge to a tiny inlet flanked by seep-stained sandstone walls. The cove is choked with willow and baccharis (or seep willow, a water-loving cousin of the sunflower) and a stream trickles from the end of the chamber. Leaves, exhaling, decomposing, dissembling as mud, perfume the dusk.

*July 29. We enter a canyon to-day, with low red walls. A short distance below its head we discover the ruins of an old building on the left wall. Its walls are of stone, laid in mortar with much regularity... Great quantities of flint chips are found on the rocks near by; and fragments of pottery are strewn about in great profusion.*

*John Wesley Powell*

At lunchtime we scrambled from the houseboat into a bowl of thistle and rock spirea and scarlet lobelia and then up a natural stairway to a second alcove where columbine trailed beneath a bottom-less pool. A more arduous way took a few zealots up another tier to redbud and oak and a shallow pond cupped by red clay. In this third alcove, cool and still as a cave, water dripped like a plucked string.

At our houseboat moored outside the little bay against a bald slope of sandstone, there are no such sensory delights. No organic musk, no ticks and drops, neither owls nor crickets nor the occasional out-of-season racketing toad. Once the springs and inlets in Glen Canyon studded a continuous ribbon of riparian habitat. Now—like the triple alcove we climbed at lunch—this cove with its mud brought down by summer floods, is one of the disconnected gardens left along the lake. Only three percent of the shoreline has soil at all; mostly, as geologist Herbert Gregory said in the 1920s of the country above the river, it is "clean bare rock."

*July 31. We have a cool, pleasant ride to-day through this part of the canyon. The walls are steadily increasing in altitude, the curves are gentle, and often the river sweeps by an arc of vertical wall, smooth and unbroken; and then by a curve that is variegated by royal arches, mossy alcoves, deep, beautiful glens, and painted grottoes.*

*John Wesley Powell*

EXCEPT FOR GLIMPSES into nooks and crannies along the reservoir, I depend on other people's images for my memory of the Glen. John Wesley Powell, the soldier-professor turned explorer, recorded the gentle beauty here as he recovered from the rigors upstream.

The Major's little fleet of wooden boats had put on the Green River at the new transcontinental rail-road bridge, 550 miles upstream, two months before. While the inexperienced oarsmen were preoccupied with negotiating a strange, wild river in unstable boats, Powell named the country—Flaming Gorge, Desolation, Labyrinth, the Glen—and carefully recorded its salient features.

Upstream of Glen Canyon, the Colorado (the Green and Grand Rivers conjoined now) cut

*August 1. ...[W]e find ourselves in a vast chamber carved out of rock. At the upper end there is a clear, deep pool of water, bordered with verdure...*
*Through the ceiling and on through the rocks for a thousand feet above, there is a narrow, winding sky-light, and this is all carved out by a little stream which runs only during the few showers that fall now and then in this arid country... When "Old Shady" sings us a song at night, we are pleased to find that this hollow in the rock is filled with sweet sounds. It was doubtless made for an academy of music by its storm-born architect; so we name it Music Temple.*

*John Wesley Powell*

prodigious rapids through the gray limestones of Cataract Canyon. Scrambling over jagged rocks in 100 degree weather, lining the heavy, heaving boats, Powell's ill-fed crew once or twice came close to brawling. Just in time, the canyon strata folded up into rosy shales and sandstones, and the scoured banks gave way to shady bottoms. The river's tumult quieted to a rustle. Powell, avid to note the transformations in the landscape, scrambled as best he could with one arm to the rim of Glen Canyon, while crewman George Bradley complained: "We are doomed to be here for another day, perhaps more than that for the Major has been making observations and seems to be no nearer done now than when he began."

After dinner, I read Powell's journal entries to my guests. Floating at dusk hundreds of feet above the old river bed, on a plane that wrinkles in the faint wind like crushed satin, we grieve time and a river stopped beneath us. Stars blossom two-fold in a mirrored sky.

# The Glen

A cool ravel
of slick silken algae
flies buzzing

tadpoles nibbling dusky mud
ferns ebony-stemmed
and emerald

water dripping stirs
a slip of a wind shivers
the sparks of columbine

leaf and water are one thing
and wind and light
one thing breathing

A Canyon off the Main Channel

# Glen Canyon: A Species List

First light
and pale buds
untwisted
by the beaks
of sphinx moths
perfume paths
stitched by
darkling beetles
around
sacred datura

All morning
blue darners
trailing
lines of
spider silk
quilt
golden weed
scarlet gilia
indian paintbrush
onto bolts
of light

Coyote willows
coppery twigs
pierced by
the pin-tipped
abdomens
of wasps
fringe
the spangled
river
red roots
tangling
under water
Say's phoebe
settling on
a wavering
stem

Red-stemmed
dogbane
paired leaves
laced by
metallic beetles
cross-stitches
noon blue sky

Scraps of color
float by
painted ladies
swallowtails
wobbling
in morning coats
out of golden
chrysalli
monarchs up
from Mexico
their ravenous
children
green and yellow
striped clowns
unraveling
the bitter milkweed

In the sheer
dusk northern
orioles knot
cats cradles
into the leaves
of cottonwoods

Drifting seeds tuft
the wet sand
Pale roots
fingering past
dark dreaming
nematodes
weave day back
into night

Escalante River

# Wild Heart

A small deer drowsing in a damp garden
of equisetum and scarlet sumac starts up
at the sudden clamor in a stillness
where boaters never come
starts up onto the thorny bench and
tangles in oak brush

Trusting that the wild can take care of themselves
we hike to an alcove scalloped with columbine
and sprawl helter-skelter on the warm stones
as if we own the place

Later when I come down alone
the little deer—his only stigmata
red dirt clotted in the fold of his velvet lip—
lays perfectly still across the new path
his coat still warm and glossy
eyes filling with clouds

San Juan side canyon

# Un-naming the Country

ON A WINDLESS AFTERNOON, Lake Powell gleams
like an enormous *tinaja* worn into stone the color
of redware. The analogy suggests stillness, a stillness flecked by the lazy drone of flies or an occasional bird call. This afternoon, though, the lake is
buzzing with Skidoos, wave runners, speedboats,
and a variety of plastic putt-putts.

The Escalante slipped through the willows and
into the heart of Glen Canyon a few hundred yards
beneath the white buoy bobbing now in the wake
of a speedboat. Powell renamed the Unknown
River after Fray Silvestre Velez de Escalante, the
journal-keeper in a little band of ten tired com-
padres who were the first Europeans to stray into
Glen Canyon.

IN OCTOBER OF 1776, Escalante's tiny party,
prompted by scant provisions and an early blizzard
in the Beaver River Valley, turned their sights from
Monterey and veered south toward the Colorado
River. Escalante reported in the expedition journal
that their mapmaker, Don Bernardo Miera, and
two others, expressed "extreme dissatisfaction" at
having to abandon their "grandiose dreams of
honor and profit." Finally after days of peevish
complaint, the good Fathers demonstrated that
God's will as expressed in the casting of lots was to
circle back to Santa Fe in Nuevo Mexico. After all,
Escalante added, "we had no other destination
than the one which God would grant us." The
sooner they regrouped, he added, the sooner they
might return to serve "the people so well disposed
to be easily gathered into the Lord's vineyard."

Guideless—their local expert skedaddled when
two of the companions broke into a pushing
match—and relying on sketchy directions in
strange tongues, they arrived two weeks later at "a
corner all hemmed in by very lofty bluffs and big

hogbacks of red earth." Soon, the route dead-ended at the mouth of the Paria, where the Echo Cliffs blocked their way upstream, and their strongest swimmers could scarcely cross the river. Their stomachs cramping on grass seeds and prickly pear and an unlucky horse, the companions scattered to search out a waist-deep ford described by the Ute Indians. After twelve soggy days spent waiting, scrambling up and down "impassible" inclines, swimming the icy river, backtracking, they found the Ute Ford thirty miles or so upstream. Splashing eagerly across, the men fired off their muskets in "great joy."

In hindsight Escalante estimated that the trip from the Beaver River—far to the north and west—across the Colorado might be made in five or six days rather than three and a half faith-tweaking weeks. Escalante reasoned that the party became lost because God was instructing them in some way.

On their two thousand-mile journey, each night's camp was named in Escalante's journal. The mouth of the Paria, where they stalled out for four days, became Paraja de San Benito Salsipuedes (*salsipuedes* means get out if you can), and their precipitous escape route up the wall of Paria canyon, Las Animas. Then came the camps of San Diego, San Carlos (where they dined on hackberry gruel), Santa Francisca Ramona, and at last at the Ute ford, La Purisima Concepcion de la Virgen Santisima. (The ford later became the Crossing of the Fathers.) When finally, by the graciousness of their Lord who decided they had learned enough, they traversed the great river, the country bore a new litany of sacred names.

MOST OF A CENTURY LATER, Navajos, harried by Kit Carson from their homelands to the east, named

*November 7. About five o'clock in the afternoon they finished crossing the river, praising God our Lord and firing off a few muskets as a sign of the great joy we all felt at having overcome so great a difficulty and which had cost us so much labor and delay, although the principal cause of our having suffered so much since we reached the Paursis was our lack of someone to guide us through such bad terrain... But doubtless God disposed that we should not obtain a guide, perhaps as a benign punishment for our sins, or perhaps in order that we might acquire some knowledge of the people who live in these parts.*

*Father. Silvestre Velez de Escalante*

the country across the Colorado from Escalante's camps for the heroes who preceeded them to their refuge; Earth Woman; Monster Slayer; Talking Rock and Spring-person. Rock-arch was a rainbow who blessed both the love-making of two sacred rivers and the subsequent births of Rain and Clouds.

*Bilagáana*, Anglos, wandering in after the War Between the States, coming for glory or gold or solitude, mapped Music Temple, Cathedral in the Desert, Reflection Canyon, Twilight, Gunsight, Forbidding, Dungeon.

Before all of these, countless names uttered in tongues I've never imagined, unwritten ever or eventually approximated by Europeans with the Roman alphabet, tossed net after net of belonging across the intricate landscape. Now the reservoir erases both the terrain and a slice of this rich map of human experience. We travel fast and heedless across a featureless plane.

# A Lament

*Put on your new boots Mangas
Colorado and we will walk down
to the river of nothing.*

Greg Pape

Ah Mangas Colorado.

Pull on your new boots
and walk with me down to the river.
Soon we'll see her flexing
her long muscles, hear her
laughing out loud.

You must be tired, Mangas Colorado
from running, from fighting.
Wade out into her cool, brown arms
and let her carry you to Mexico.

Ah Mangas Colorado, lo siento.
I must have been dreaming.

The river is drowned.
This river is nothing.


Bald Rock Canyon


Mangas Colorado, A Chiricahua Apache, vanished time and again
into Mexico during a long, tragic fight for his homeland above the
border. Although the Apache are kin to the Navajo, Mangas Colorado
never came this far north. Pape's "river of nothing" is southern
Arizona's plundered Santa Cruz.

# The Reservoir

*Here in Glen Canyon
we had plenty of mud,
for the river had been
falling the last few
days... The willows
and dense shrubbery
came down close to the
river; the mud was
black, deep, and
sticky; all driftwood
had gone out on the
last flood. Meanwhile
a glorious full moon
had risen, spreading a
soft, weird light over
the canyon walls and
the river.*

*Ellsworth Kolb*

IN 1911 Emery and Ellsworth Kolb, keen to shoot a
moving picture of the Colorado River for tourists at
the South Rim of Grand Canyon, made their "Big
Trip" from Green River, Wyoming to Mexico. The
brothers relished their chats with the work-hard-
ened men who dropped out here and again along
the river—at Cass Hite's place at the head of the
Glen a prospecting river runner named Bert Loper
told them only one woman had visited there in the
last twelve years. Glen Canyon was just as quiet
when the Kolbs returned in 1921 to guide an expedition to identify potential dam sites co-sponsored
by the United States Geological Survey and
California Edison.

A year later the preliminary survey maps were
the basis for preparing the Colorado River
Compact, an agreement apportioning the water of
the Colorado between its upper and lower basin
states. In 1953 when a proposal arose to dam the
Green River in Dinosaur National Monument as
water storage for the upper basin states, raising the
dam already sketched in for the little-known Glen
Canyon was offered as an alternative. Just ten years
later Glen Canyon Dam was complete, a sweep of
concrete rising 710 feet above bedrock, flaring from
a 350 foot wide base to a crest that curves 1560
feet from canyon wall to canyon wall.

Whole rivers rollicking down the west face of
the Rockies finally brimmed along nearly two thousand miles of finely branched shoreline at the
planned elevation of 3700 feet. The silt carried by
the many-limbed Colorado—notorious for being
too thick to drink and too thin to plow—dropped
out when the current slowed and then stopped,
molding new profiles in muck at the mouths of side
streams, blanketing the lakebed. The reservoir,
pooled from cliff to cliff, wells clear and cold and
dead still across the old topographic relief.

In 1983 heavy May snows and a quick thaw surprised the dam managers, and spillways opened for the first time were battered by spring torrents. Crumbling Navajo sandstone spewed out of the spillways and into the green river churning through the dam's outlets. With the spillways closed, the reservoir threatened to pour over the low gates on each side of the dam. Sheets of 4-by-8 plywood, erected above the gates by a desperate dam crew, held back the top few feet of the reservoir, raising its surface temporarily to 3708 feet above sea level.

IN THE GLEN the rhythmic changes of a desert river, surging when the snow melts in the Rocky Mountains, slowed to a trickle in the fall and winter, bumptiously unpredictable in the summer, were turned inside out by human desires. Air-conditioning, city lights, strategic water-hoarding dictate Lake Powell water levels which one year drown out established shrubs and trees, and another desiccate water-lovers like willow and baccharis. Even where there is a pocket of soil, plants evolved with the old rhythms have a hard time coping with the sporadic changes.

Still, wild nature is prepared for drastic change and a new clientele lurks in the wings. Tamarisk, an imported weed with a genius for colonizing wet sand, dominates the beach we're parked at tonight, one of the scattered sandy coves along the main channel. Averse to sleeping in houseboats, I thread my way through the tammies with my bedroll, avoiding the copses with little knots of toilet paper emerging at the roots. Forty years ago, I'd have made my bed "down there" in an untidy, many-storied aviary of cottonwood—or boxelder—sandbar willow and tree-sized Goodding willow, rhus and rabbit-brush and bunch grass. Tonight I sleep under the wispy branches of the tamarisk on a beach suspended halfway up a slickrock dome, just below the stars.

Instead of waking to bugs buzzing and the murmurations of birds, I tiptoe down to the houseboat in an eerie stillness punctuated by the occasional thrum of a settling pontoon.

As DAMS AND CATTLE and bulldozers decimate the locals, tamarisk, like cheatgrass and other misplaced opportunists, exploits the changed habitat. The natives fine-tuned their habits, generation by generation, to occupy a particular niche in their close-knit neighborhood. The immigrants, free-wheeling generalists with no sense of history, provide meager support for the old gall-forming, leaf-gobbling, egg-laying creatures who once were feasts for birds and toads and fish. The coming of the outsiders, like the reservoir which empowers them, signals a simplification, a narrowing of possibility, a blanding of the landscape.

# The New Lake

Jayne the dancer who rows boats
saw the brilliant blue lake
and dreamed the sky had fallen.

It's done with mirrors I told her.

This is not sky—air plaiting
brilliant air or spinning
into thermals marked
by hawks and dry leaves.

And clearly it's no river that pours
over rocks and circles back,
flow and flux whispering
on the scales of fishes and
cottonseed drifting and silver sticks.

Nothing stirs here now
without gasoline or hard work.

Nothing licks the backs of stones
or swirls light down a bubble line
or talks with the walking rain.

This is not the sky.
This is not a river.

This is sleight of hand,
illusion,
no place.


Lake Powell

# The Unhaunting

This is like swimming with ghosts
she whispered. Ah but the ghosts are long gone.

Once the nights—electric with stars or cloud-damped—
creaked and muttered and sighed.

On summer afternoons small winds skimmed off
the river's gleaming spine and spiraled into dustdevils.

Mysteries stirred in coiling water
in the sleek bodies of mud-breathing fishes
in boulders yielding to silk.

But when the lake drowned the thickets and
backeddies and shaded cutbanks
and settled like dread on their airy shoulders
the breath bodies fled.

This water weighs too heavy too still.
Even the fishes are trying to leave.

All night they hurl their thick hearts into the sky
and fall back swaying beneath our boat.


Lake Powell

# The Heart of the Matter

The old river sliced down through our stratiform
hearts, revealing the lenses of delight—
cool desert nights, skin on skin, bright-eyed babies—
and wind-blown, crosswise layers of loss,
all the things that can never be again.

Closer to base level she dropped our night
dreads and dead ends, our heavy metals
onto her bed of mud and cobbles.

An August flood would surely break the snarls apart,
dilute the poisons, swirl the detritus downriver,
wrack and feast for ravens or noon-fire,
or the next thunderbuster.

Ah, but this river is damned.
We are stuck, stranded.

How then will our breath bodies float free?
How will they come back as rain?


Glen Canyon Dam

# Letting Go the River

THERE'S A MOVE AFOOT to undo Lake Powell. Some day, of course, the river will go on down on her own, melting the porous sandstone beneath the concrete massif or silting up the reservoir like those beaver-ponds-turned-to-sandy-thickets off the Escalante. I'm not talking about the river's will, though, but human will, and according to some, God's as well. I'm talking about "decommissioning" the dam, a bit of jargon arrived at by a handful of heartfelt eccentrics at the heart of a radical movement. They propose with a passion that belies the terminology that we not wait for Earth Woman to undo a grievous human error.

Protests from the humans who make a living, or part of a life, in the current Glen Canyon ecosystem—power and water brokers, purveyors of wave runners, bass fisherman and beaming, sunburned families—do not faze these zealots. Nor do the reasoned arguments of social philosophers of one school or another, nor the scientists' admonitions that it's too soon for an informed decision. Although proponents promise an Environmental Impact Statement before the floodgates open and the river flows through, surely their hearts will not be changed by data.

Parked for the evening at the end of the Waterpocket Fold, our little party watches the autumn light incandesce on the cliffs across the channel. A breeze transmutes the water to flakes of copper. Despite the universe of Navajo sandstone inviting us up from our scruffy beach, we sit, beers in hand, around a roll-a-table, imagining the emptying of the reservoir. I tell these folks about Lake Pagahrit up by Halls Crossing, created when blow sand and sediments created a natural dam across a side canyon more than sixty feet high. Eight decades after the obstacle flushed out, the canyon is messy but lush with beaver ponds and full-grown cottonwoods. Despite my story, most of our little group sensibly decides that decommissioning is a bad idea; too many people—including us—have too much to lose.

And indeed what would we gain, our little houseboat crew? Downstream in Grand Canyon, the disruption of a maturing new order and a three-quarter-turn toward a more demanding, less predictable equilibrium. Up in the Glen, mud, red mud slicked over black; mud-plastered ruins, mud-encased trash; rusted gas tanks, pontoons, batteries; battered jet skis; toilet seats, toilet tanks, toilet contents; beer cans and oil cans; the remains of hikers, cows, cottonwoods; heavy metals; radioactive wastes. The detritus of a high-tech society and locals with no trash collection service, of built environments and un-built ones, borne downstream and piled up in Eden.

AH, BUT THERE'S Earth Woman. Won't she, after all, hurl down her male rain, unfurl waterfalls, purify by light? Past the thorns and thickets, the jagged edges and putrefaction, the other changes we can scarcely imagine, a stream will slip—or hurtle—by, muttering and silking, undercutting the banks, carrying off the stuff. Seeds will germinate, most of them into appalling weeds, but datura too, perfuming the night from the hems of south-facing walls. Gnats and mosquitoes will reel in pallid bats and the stone-nesters—black phoebes, canyon wrens. The last giant pikeminnows, will power upstream to spawn where fingerlings can drift down from backwater to backwater. Woodhouse's toads will plop out on spring nights to bleat for sex. When the willows sprout, the beaver will come. And maybe my granddaughters or their daughters will float and daydream and sing at night under deep blue sherds of sky shot through with stars.

*Flowering Plants of Glen Canyon*

*sandbar willow · baccharis · hackberry · cottonwood · box elder · horsetail · cattail · bullrush · Indian rice grass · alkali sacaton · drop seed · tall reed · common reed · wildrose · squawbush · greasewood · rabbitbrush · narrow-leaved yucca · blackbrush · hedgehog · prickly pear · sand sage · indigo bush · virgin bower · single leaf ash · false tarragon · liverwort · dogbane · redbud · false solomon seal · stream orchid · maidenhair fern · columbine · monkey flower · Easter flower · rock spirea · cardinal flower · speedwell · giant thistle · sego lily · buckwheat · prickly poppy · prince's plume · lupine · locoweed · globe mallow · blazing star · gilia · sacred datura · penstemon · paintbrush · goldenaster · goldenrod · fleabane · mulesears · blanketflower · sunflower*

*Mammals of*
*Glen Canyon*

*Yuma myotis ·*
*small-footed myotis ·*
*western pipestrelle ·*
*black-tailed jackrabbit ·*
*desert cottontail · rock*
*squirrel · antelope*
*ground squirrel ·*
*chipmunk · silky pocket*
*mouse · harvest mouse ·*
*canyon mouse · deer*
*mouse · pinyon mouse ·*
*grasshopper mouse ·*
*kangaroo rat ·*
*white-throated wood*
*rat · bushy-tailed*
*wood rat · beaver ·*
*porcupine ·*
*coyote · red fox · grey*
*fox · ringtail cat ·*
*raccoon · long-tailed*
*weasel · badger · spotted*
*skunk · bobcat · mule*
*deer · bison ·*
*mountain sheep*

IN THEIR SACRUM, their holy bone, the ones here who have been waltzed down a free-flowing stream know that were they asked to cast a vote, a secret ballot, yea or nay, to let go the river, their only choice is yes. In *Biophilia*, E. O. Wilson reminds us of the eternal, internal tug-of-war between the garden and the machine, our need to control, our need for Earth Woman to do her thing. We tipped the balance too far in Glen Canyon, the dam-building impulse fueled by a compelling gut stew of fear and optimism. We ravished Eden, not to survive, but to make our lives more secure and more sumptuous. From our sacrum, though, our heart, our blood, wherever the tides of conscience rise, we hear this urging forty years later; make it right.

Reason says give me the facts, skimpy as our knowledge of ecosystems may be, and let me make my decision on solid grounds. Reason says don't assume right is on your side just because you eschew combustion engines in the wilderness. The poet says I hear you Reason, but I vote, perched metaphorically on a quaking patch of quicksand, to bring back the garden. I have this stunning body of water to lose and nothing, save perhaps my soul's well-being, to gain. Still, for my species, garden obligates as well as splendid inventors, I vote yes. Because altruism is going extinct, I vote yes. Because I hope my grandchildren's world will be complicated and mysterious and unfettered, yes. In the name of dreams, for the toads and treefrogs and humpback chub, and with sympathy for the disinherited, yes. And, of course, for the river.

*Birds of Glen Canyon*

*snowy egret · great
blues · Canada goose ·
teal · lesser goldeneye ·
western grebe · coot ·
turkey vulture · red-
tailed hawk · golden
eagle · prairie falcon ·
peregrine · kestrel ·
raven · mourning
dove · killdeer · peeps ·
poor-will · nighthawk ·
great-horned owl ·
white-throated swift ·
cliff swallow · violet-
green swallow · broad-
tailed hummingbird ·
black-chinned
hummingbird · belted
kingfisher · red-shafted
flicker · yellow-bellied
sapsucker · Cassin's
kingbird · olive-sided
flycatcher · ash-throated
flycatcher · Say's phoebe
· horned lark · scrub
jay · raven · water
ouzel · canyon wren ·*

*rock wren · robin ·
blue-gray
gnatcatcher · Lucy's
warbler · yellow
warbler · yellowthroat ·
yellow-breasted chat ·
yellow-headed black-
bird · northern oriole ·
western tanager · blue
grosbeak · lazuli
bunting · rufous-sided
towhee · lark
sparrow · black-throated
sparrow · sage sparrow ·
white-crowned
sparrow · song sparrow*

*Adapted from
"The Place No One Knew"*

# Cycles

Sand stilled, or clay or silt, dropped by the wind,
by a sea, tired for a while of wandering,
settled into darkness and buried, became stone,
every grain dense with memory and dreams,
the spaces between humming.

When the stone folded and opened to a river,
waves of sand spun off the eddy lines
and light, kindled on new beaches,
lifted into the clouds
that exhaled the silver gusts of rain
that hiss and polish and open stone.

Now this imposter of a sea, the sinking-
not-rising, flow stopped, willows
drowned, deep tongues of silt slipping
back into the dark.

Still, the reservoir hangs a thousand metres
above the sea's true level,
and with every year's turning
there is the pillowed snow, a swirling
mutter of rain, water's
inexorable weight
and memory
and dream.

Lake Powell

# Another Glen

ON A PERFECT fall morning, I'm hiking south toward the Colorado along the edge of an enormous fold in the earth's crust. Paralleling the Escalante to the north and east, this sandy creekbed offered an easy walk into the Glen for Fremont farmers, and Utes and Paiutes, and for the Anglos when they finally found it. The Glen Canyon formations are stacked underfoot here and to the east, but a sudden wrinkle in the strara thrusts them up diagonally on my right hand.

Although the wagon road continues along the base of the uplift, an abrupt meander in the creek plunges me into the heart of Navajo sandstone. The way turns cool and narrow. Gardens glossed by algae and pillowed with mosses and drifts of maidenhair fern hang in the bends of the canyon. The mud underfoot is mostly water, the water mostly mud; both are the color of flower pots. Light floats like pink smoke between walls patinated blue-black, or tiger-striped with salt and iron. A thousand feet overhead blue ribbon of sky twists in a far off breeze. Despite being swayed at first by the slick-rock mounds and monuments, in the end Powell named Glen Canyon for secret gardens like this one. A friend recommended this narrows to me as a relic of the smoothed-over world down the creek from here.

MY DICTIONARY defines a glen as a secluded narrow valley, and there were plenty branching off from the larger canyon of the Colorado, but Powell expanded the pastoral Scottish term to include the hanging gardens tucked in hollows in the sandstone. Seeping down through the porous, lithified sand dunes, water deflects off lenses of less permeable stone— the floor of an old, clay-lined stream channel, or the limey accumulation on a desert lakebed—and moves sideways until it escapes at the canyon wall.

*August 2. We have a curious ensemble of wonderful features— carved walls, royal arches, glens, alcove gulches, mounds, and monuments. From which of these features shall we select a name? We decide to call it Glen Canyon.*

*August 3. The river, sweeping around these bends, undermines the cliffs in places. Sometimes the rocks are overhanging; in other curves, curious, narrow glens are found. Through these we climb, by a rough stairway, perhaps several hundred feet, to where a spring bursts out from under an overhanging cliff and where cottonwoods and willows stand, while along the curves of the brooklet oaks grow and other rich vegetation is seen. We call these Oak Glens.*

*John Wesley Powell*

Spores from algae and moss and ferns drift in from-who-knows-where and colonize the damp stone, the new lives foreshadowing a handful of humus. Seeds arrive on the wind or with the droppings of birds and germinate in the patches of detritus; their roots and the water wear away at the rock.

Each glen has its cast of characters, depending on its aspect, the chance journeys of spores and seeds, local chemistry. In September, scarlet lobelia still wink at me from the green frieze and a few late blooming mimulus, their leaves smelling of cedar wood. In other gardens I have seen tiny salmon-colored orchids, purple Easter flowers, mats of rock spirea, and that Alice-in-Wonderland prickler, Rydberg thistle, which like the Easter flowers grows only in this neighborhood.

These tapestries-contained-in-sculptures were Glen Canyon's art forms. A far cry from the reflecting pool downstream, each intricate piece was created by a scant measure of nature's elixer.

Today I'm making the most of my usual sweep's position to dawdle and daydream through the narrows. Well behind my companions and fooled by the opaque red water, I stumble into a chest-high pool. When I emerge from the moss-streaked corridor and join the little group oohing over a lithic scatter, I'm dripping and dyed to match the landscape.

THE NEXT DAY we hike to Lake Powell, scuffling across a sun-blasted, lake-bleached floodplain, threading through thornbushes, and at the edge, waist-high tammies. We're leaving paradise by speedboat. With a roar and a relentless whap-whap across the waves, we hurtle toward the marina.

Navajo Mountain and the Rainbow Plateau

# Navajo Mountain

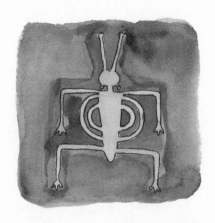

POWELL FIRST MAPPED the rounded peak at the
heart of the Glen Canyon basin as Mount Seneca
Howland, after one of three men who hiked out of
the Grand Canyon on Powell's first river expedition only to be murdered on the North Rim. The
name never stuck though, and in 1912 Ellsworth
Kolb wrote of "...Navajo Mountain, a sandstone
peak, towering 7000 feet above the river...[its] base
rounded and gullied into curious forms..." The

*Head Mountain!*
*Head Mountain!*
*Naatsis'áán!*
*Naatsis'áán!*
*Black Wind, splendid*
*Chief!*
*From the tips of your*
*fingers a rainbow*
*put out.*
*Thrust a rainbow*
*from your brow,*
*A rainbow from the*
*palm of your hand—*
*By which let me walk.*
*Black Wind and black*
*clouds,*
*Blue Wind and blue*
*clouds,*
*Yellow Wind and*
*yellow clouds,*
*White Wind and*
*clouds of white—*
*Go thou all before me*
*and darken the sun.*
*Wrapped in your cloud*
*garments let me*
*walk.*
*With your garments of*
*clouds about me.*

Navajos who arrived in the area not long before
Powell, when the mountain was still Paiute territory,
have their own name, Naatsis'áán.

One May, I hike dudes down to Rainbow Bridge
through the "curious forms" sweeping up from the
confluence of the Colorado and the San Juan.
Heading around the mountain on the Rainbow
Plateau, a dissected bench of Navajo sandstone, I
hardly remember that there is a lake down there, or
even that the twentieth century has arrived.
Despite the trampling by burros and sheep,
Naatsis'áán's terrain, a remote slice of the Navajo
Nation, remains largely unchanged since Major
Powell's men floated by in 1872.

J.W. Powell's men conducted their Survey of the
Colorado River Country across the river from
Navajo Mountain. Except for prospectors greedy for
silver, and nineteenth-century adventurers led by
guides to Rainbow Bridge, EuroAmericans,
*bilagáana*, haven't often explored this side of Glen
Canyon. Although tourists ogle the Bridge from the
lakeshore now, permission from the Navajo Nation
is still required to hike this far country.

WHEN I PESTER HIM for his stories about this other
world, our Navajo guide grins that everyone has
their own and they are all true. An Anglo, I heard
these things in class: the laccolithic mountain was
created by magma folding up layers of country rock;

the Navajo are newcomers who elbowed into what was Paiute territory in the 1850s, when Hoskininni and his family were harried there by Ute and New Mexican slave traders.

Local stories, though, recount how holy beings shaped the mountain around a light-filled inner form using soil brought from a previous world. And oral tradition asserts Naatsis'áán and her Rainbow Plateau, lying within the fork of two sacred rivers, as ancestral Navajo homeland. Although the Paiutes lived here when the Diné arrived, the holy people had come long before, marking the territory.

Largely from scholars' re-tellings, I have gleaned that Naatsis'áán is the head of Earth Woman, a figure sprawling across the high desert south of the San Juan; Black Mesa to the south and east is her body and Agathla, a volcanic neck near Monument Valley, her wool spindle. Monster Slayer, the son of Changing Woman and the Sun, lived for a time in a flint hogan atop the Mountain. His life and death struggle with He Who Kicks People Off took place at Naatsis'áán. It was Monster Slayer who used his shield to stop the spruce and pine trees Black God threw this way from Dook'o'oslííd (the San Francisco Peaks) and who planted them on the stony slopes.

The natural bridge at the base of the mountain is reputed here to be two rainbows, male and female. These rainbow people, the two great rivers making love nearby, and the sacred springs on the mountain all gave birth to water children, to the clouds and rain.

Anglo and Navajo histories agree that in the 1860s the number of local Diné swelled to more than a thousand as Navajos fleeing Kit Carson's raiders disappeared into the maze of canyons at the foot of Navajo Mountain. They managed to escape the Long Walk to Fort Sumner, despite the federal

*Let it rain peacefully
  before me,
Let the corn ripen—
The White corn,
  the Yellow and
  the Blue.
Earth Woman, send
  the rain...
Now all is happiness.
Now all is happiness.*

*Slim Woman*

troops manning the heliograph station at the summit. Local folk say that the Navajos hiding from the soldiers were protected by Earth Woman herself and by Monster Slayer's shield.

USUALLY A GUIDE escorts her folks all the way out of strange terrain. This Canyonlands Field Institute group jets away across the reservoir while Karla, my boss, and I wave goodbye from the Park Service's floating dock below Rainbow Bridge. Shades of John Wetherill, the trader from Kayenta whose curious, indefatigable spirit goaded him time and again into the maze of stone behind Naatsis'áán, we're riding up from the stone rainbow on horseback.

John's wife and business partner, Louisa, was fluent in Navajo—speaking the language, she wrote, made home home. She learned of the natural bridge deep in the outback from her Navajo friends. The story of the bridge spread among the Anglos, and soon both archeologist Byron Cummings and government surveyor William Douglass were chafing to find it.

In 1901, Wetherill, a model of both diplomacy and backcountry savvy, rode with Navajo Nasja Begay and Mike's Boy, a Paiute, to lead these old antagonists to the stone wonder. Cummings and Douglass were each eager to claim the "discovery," but Wetherill—who pointed out that the Indians had always known the rainbow made manifest— managed to defuse the expedition's egos with his calm, good sense.

Eric, our horsepacker-guide and an aspiring land-use planner, leads the way up from the marvel this morning. My stomach clenched all night imagining this adventure, but fortunately I'm riding Frank, a wise and agile Navajo pony. Frank scrambles up slickrock pitches so steep his hooves slide, picks his hard-footed way along the sides of

*It was hard work picking our way down the bed of the creek, which was formed of slippery painful rocks. The trail slipped through clumps of willows and oaks; always it led around another bend... Supper was entirely a canned one, as we hurried through it...hoping before night fell to catch a glimpse of the wonder... Around the first bend in the canyon we saw it—Nonne-zoche... Gradually the reds, the blues, the yellows, the grays, the purples in the rock faded and blended into deepest ebony. It was night, and the Bridge, which in the sunset had symbolized the Glory of Nature, the Reward of Toil and Vibrant*

cliffs, jumps from ledges and kicks over cobbles.
Settling deeper in the saddle, I learn to lean forward uphill, to lower my heels alongside Frank's
chest going down.

Black hair swinging halfway to his waist, Eric
sings in Navajo. From the stone rainbow where we
parted from our guests, we ride up the streambed
past our last night's camp in the spring-worn alcove
furnished with rusted bedsteads. Eventually turning
east, the disintegrating CCC trail, ball bearinged
with cobbles, heads across the canyons. We wind
through sleeves of wildflowers (for awhile I wheedle
Navajo names from Eric, names I can't remember)
and along sandstone cliffs that sheer now above our
heads, now hundreds of feet below our ponies' feet.
My fear of falling evaporates into the rock-edged
frames of blue sky and towering black clouds, into
wind gusts and stillness and flies buzzing in the
noon sun. As naive as the good father Escalante,
I feel cradled by the country.

Eric tells me that before the reservoir filled, his
family forded the Colorado, to graze their horses in
the canyons of the Escalante or to hunt or gather
plants on the Kaiparowits. Although the risks
inherent in crossing out of Diné Tah required a
protection ceremony, beyond the rivers the frontier
was spacious and grass abundant. Despite the
drowning of the old trails, from Frank's back the
Navajo world still seems endless. Apparently
untroubled, Eric sings all the way to the corral.

*Passion, was now
majestic and omnipo-
tent Eternity;
all the mystery and
immutability of Fate
were typified in that
blackest curve. The
moon rose. Nonne-
zoche lost its hardness
and in the soft light
was again wondrous
and sylph-like—Young
Love, Dreams, Sweet
Music, the Beauty of
Quiet Places.*

*Clyde Kluckhohn*

*I am spared.
I am spared.
Enemy has missed me,
enemy has missed me.
Today it did not
    happen,
today it did not
    happen.*

*Ernest Nelson*

# Topography

At the canyon's rim we looked out
over the center of the earth.

In the four directions:
the dark head of Pollen Woman,
her hair flowing; the Rainbow Plateau;
pink Paiute Mesa and the red sweep of Wilson;
Waterpocket Fold's white ribs; the maroon curves
of the Circle Cliffs; Escalante's umbral, knotted gorge;
the far, strict cliffs of the Kaiparowits.
In each direction rock, shadow and sky.
Beneath us blue, startling blue,
the azure of the Aegean.

Going down at evening, on an overslung
boulder on the Chinle bench, a lone,
precisely-pecked desert bighorn
says this is still dry country.

Neskahi

# Patterns

THE CANYONLANDS FIELD INSTITUTE folks who
zoomed away from Rainbow Bridge were landscape architects, and I'm a gardener too in my
other life. The pleasure they took in Earth
Woman's patterns matches my own. Water and
aridity, yin and yang, tend her beds. Aridity clears
the pale ground, bare expanses with little to hold
the sand in place. Precipitation—a meager six or
so inches a year falling in summer thunderbusters
and winter snow and rain—shapes the topography,
rearranging sandflats in a flash, worrying away at
stone for centuries. And these two, moisture and
aridity, dictate who lives where; clumps of pinyons
and their laughing jays, their mice and woodrats
and tree lizards here; grasses and kangaroo rats
there.

Up on the cooler brow of the mountain, where
winter snows accumulate and evaporation is slow,
the firs and spruces thrown by Black God from
the San Francisco Peaks flourish. Down here on
the Rainbow Plateau, shade, soil, substrate—
largely elements which husband water—arrange
Earth Woman's desert habitats in a mosaic.

Swaths of pinyon pine and juniper finger down
from higher, more accommodating country on
shaded exposures and along washes. Singleleaf ash
and three-leaf sumac send their roots into watered
cracks of sandstone. Yellow mulesears daisies and
indigo bush thrive on sand dune aquifers and hold
the world together when the wind howls. At
warmer elevations, redbud trees, flamboyant now
when they are all flowers and no leaves, grace the
springs and wetter creekbeds.

As our little band rested on the hike down to
the Stone-Arch, I read to them from anthropologist
Clyde Kluckhohn's account of "the last stronghold
of Virgin Nature." In the 1920s, on his horseback
trip to the foot of the Rainbow, he marvels at how

*The atmosphere
seemed entirely new; it
had a peculiar reaction
upon our olfactory
organs... grass had
been short and scarce
heretofore, but here it
was green and luxuri-
ant, waist-high; there
were the rare orchid-
like sego lilies—at first
only the white ones;
then as we dropped
lower in approaching
the level of the
Colorado the delicate
yellow and pink ones
appeared; the purple
sage, which grows only
in this region, was
conspicuous ...*

*Clyde Kluckhohn*

Nature's garden evolves as it rounds the Mountain to the cooler north flank.

In the Navajo universe, order and chaos balance one another. On Earth Woman's undisturbed flank, high above the reservoir, order prevails. Her watering systems and her landscape design bespeak efficiency and continuance. Indeed all her patterns— her gardens, the shapes of her terrain, the flow of energy manifested in wild creatures—feel healthy and whole, despite the exotic weeds encroaching at her feet.

Resourceful locals have always relied on Nature's tutelage to garden successfully in dry country, saving seeds, seeking out and making the most of freely-offered moisture, encouraging companion plants. Despite a new enthusiasm for natives, urban gardeners largely ignore the constraints of home—as well as the rewards of neighborly collaboration. I order in flats of bright exotic flowers and pipe my water from a reservoir. My seeds are grown in other ecosystems and make plants without viable seeds of their own. I go to a nursery to buy dirt and food and occasionally even poisons for my garden. Seduced by trade goods, I forget my place and the well-being that comes with nestling in.

# Circles

*There are whorls here at the tips of our fingers. Winds stick out here. It is the same way on the toes of our feet… Winds exist on us… where there are spirals… These whorls at the tips of our toes hold us to the Earth. Those at our fingertips hold us to the Sky. Because of these, we do not fall when we move about.*

CM, *a Navajo Singer*

The spirals on my fingertips, the curled
shell of my ear, are traces of the holy wind
who breathes us all to life.

She strokes
my cheek and I soften in my sleeping bag
like a baby snuggling to a breast.

These sighs and ticks and rustlings
are night sounds from another home
out on the open grasslands.

Distances
nurture me, stone flowing into shadow
and everything shivering, stars,
rice grass, clouds.

Time circles like
a whirlwind. I am two and ten and fifteen
and fifty. A wandering poet, a space
cowboy, a gatherer of seeds.

Navajo Mountain

*Far in the east,*
*  far below there*
*  a house*
*  was made;*
*Beautiful house.*
*God of Dawn,*
*  there his house*
*  was made;*
*Beautiful house...*
*Water in plenty*
*  surrounding,*
*  for it a house*
*  was made;*
*Beautiful house.*
*Corn pollen,*
*  for it a house*
*  was made;*
*Beautiful house.*
*The ancients make*
*  their presence*
*  beautiful;*
*Beautiful house.*

*A Navajo Song*
*Recorded by Cosmos*
*Mindeleff*

UNDER A FIESTA-BLUE bowl of a sky, a handful of Four Corners School hikers records rock art south of the San Juan at the base of Navajo Mountain. Our leader, archeologist Don Keller, reports our accomplishments to the Navajo Nation. Don, a reincarnation perhaps of that weathered Quaker trader John Wetherill, arms us with maps and clipboards and sends us scattering up dry streambeds and over sandrock divides. One of our survey crew, a city guy from the Bay Area, marvels, "You feel like you're in the middle of nowhere until you find a drawing and then you know you're somewhere."

Before Glen Canyon Dam's floodgates were closed, salvage archeologists hurried over the basin recording the remains of past cultures. Fanning out along the creekbeds, they found thousands of signs of a scattered prehistoric people; piled rock, pot sherds, scatters of stone flakes, the blackened earth of hearth fires. What established villages and fields the Ancestral Puebloans (Anasazi) left fell along the once arable, now largely drowned, terraces just off the river—Powell noted ruins above the mouths of White and Red Canyons—but the traces of their comings and goings are up here above the shore of the Reservoir too. Like their four-legged and winged neighbors, humans here have always lived lightly, their adaptations to place so subtle and so myriad that we who embrace development on a grand scale can scarcely conceive of them.

Our first morning we followed a sinuous channel carved into Kayenta sandstone, the layer of reworked river sands sandwiched between the lithified dunes of the Navajo and Wingate formations. On a living dune above the wash, among widely spaced clumps of Mormon tea and Indian rice grass, we discovered the spare remains of a Basketmaker gathering camp; blackened dirt and scattered slabs of sandstone, some half-buried on their edges, others worn concave from manos pushed back and forth across their surfaces, grinding seeds.

The Basketmakers brought corn from Mexico millennia ago. These hunting-and-gathering seasonal farmers lived frugally, accepting with equanimity and alacrity what the earth provided, never presuming to control her largesse in any serious way. The seasons of their lives were marked in the ripening of seed, the swelling of pine nuts.

The Puebloans, descendants of the Basketmakers, hiked these canyons until they left for good in the late 1200s. Settled deeper into farming, they depended more on crops, crops that needed planting, tending, worrying over, rain. Still, "the genius of the Anasazi lay in… ancient foraging skills to which was added horticulture" according to Jesse Jennings, director of the University of Utah survey. He called these folk "typical backwoods Anasazi" who "specialized in gardening in marginal areas, and, by understanding water and its conservation and use (and the idiosyncracies of their crops), extended their domain into areas where neither then nor now is gardening truly feasible."

TODAY WE'RE SURVEYING in a canyon farther up the San Juan, where the Chinle swamp deposits underlying the Wingate sandstone are exposed by the Monument Upwarp. We leave our tired-looking camp with its litter of driftwood, oil bottles, an occasional sneaker, and hike uphill to a spring beneath an enormous cottonwood, an oasis today for the Navajo's feral cows and a thousand years ago for Puebloan farmers. The rest of the day we'll wander a high terrace eroded from the clay slopes of the Chinle, searching for rock art and shade.

The high, holy, hotter-than-Hades benches offer long views ending in red escarpments, shadow mountains. The terrace is strewn with massive, straight-sided slabs, taller than houses, churches even, thrown out from sheer Wingate walls and blackened by desert varnish; slates for travelers, hunters and gatherers, Navajo cowboys.

One monolith is pecked with a lively intaglio of small figures: ducks, tracks of rabbit and deer and bear, a snake, lizard men and men with birds for heads. Pressed by my companions to "explain," I recall that ducks in pueblo myth bind together earth and sky and water; that the Zunis speak of First Man as lizard; that shamans often call upon animal helpers, but what do I know really? These folk belonged deep in a magical, delicately-balanced universe, in which everything had spirit and everyone—two-legged or four or six, scaled or feathered—was connected. Even here, up to our shins in snakeweed in this hot, brilliant light, it is a faraway place.

## Making a Home

At the confluence of two ephemeral creeks
the country is deep and green. We scramble
along a crack onto a shoulder of Wingate,
contour to a side canyon, and zigzag up
and up to the divide.
                              A camp
hunkered against a fin of sandstone,
three small rooms carelessly drawn
with piled stone. A makeshift shelter
strewn with four hundred years
of finely painted pottery.
                              Kneeling,
we turn the fragments in our fingers,
stroking the designs, sketching them.
In front of us pink sand slopes
away to a faint green wash, another fin,
a swell of sky lapping
at our feet.
                    And what of the people
who carried these pots, cool surfaces
gleaming, into every cranny
of this empty place?
                         Men and women walking
wove this far-flung landscape into home.
No hearth to speak of, no tables,
no chairs, just gardens, each other,
smoothed and painted clay,
stars, stone, stories.


A Divide

# Tracks

*I distrust ever return-*
*ing to the cities. Here*
*I wander in beauty*
*and perfection. There*
*one walks in the midst*
*of ugliness and mis-*
*takes. All is made for*
*man, but where can*
*one find surrounding*
*to match one's ideals*
*and imaginings?*

*Everett Ruess*

To SAY NOTHING has changed here since Powell's day is foolish, of course. Everything has, change being what life is, and everything here being vibrantly alive. Comings and goings are written everywhere—half-circles inscribed by wind-tossed rice grass, a line of hand-sized bird tracks pecked on a boulder—and human footprints are uncommon, interesting. Someone came this way, how curious, what were they up to? A sandal track engraved in desert varnish centuries ago inspires the same questions.

In the Chinle hills above Paiute Canyon, burro tracks are the only common ones. The greedy gnomes, scattered in little bands of two or three— wiry things with shaggy manes and big eyes—eat every blessed thing they can digest. Everett Ruess, the young romantic on a fatal quest for beauty, wandered over Earth Woman's terrain with his own burros in the 1930s. The beasts always know the way, my friend says; "el burro sabe mas que tu", and their tracks make good trails over the jumbled mounds of orange cobbles and lavender clay.

A little band of hikers eager for a view from the rim of the cliffs rising above the burro's terraces, as well as for rock art, heads out after lunch. We fol- low one of the lightly traveled trails that link the Rainbow Plateau with springs and camps in the canyons. No doubt this route was pioneered thou- sands of years ago and improved ever so slightly by the Ancestors, a step carved here, a tree branch leaned up there.

Navajos, more recently, made it useful for cows and sheep by piling stones in dips, arranging juniper skeletons to fence a perilous curve. Elegantly sim- ple, exactly fitted to the terrain, the path unfurls underfoot, step by mindful step. Zigzagging up and up on this subtle trail, my monkey mind kicks in, and, fretting about an old mistake, I lose the thread on one washed-out stretch. My little band unravels on a precarious-looking jumble of rock looking for the way. When we're in a tidy line again, passing a faded soda can I remember stuck on a branch two years ago, I second the Navajo respect for light-mindedness—the ability to eschew worry and sentimentality for the here and now.

Catching our breaths on a rubbled switchback we contemplate the Navajo wisdom about walking in beauty. A loose translation for *Bik' eh Hózho̱*, the refrain signifies, as best English can, moving in synch through an ordered, beautiful, humming-along world. Full and harmonious participation in Earth Woman's ongoing creation. On this trail to the Rainbow Plateau, even twenty-first century urbanites seem to get it.

Today's route twists ingeniously up a talus slope and the sheer-faced Wingate sandstone, and tops out above a perched valley. Doubling back down the streambed, a carefully pieced stone ramp bypasses the dry waterfall and leads to the tinaja beneath it. Above the ramp a weathered, hand-turned chair leg is tucked into a cranny in the rock, helpful no doubt for urging animals down to water.

One faint set of Nike tracks, imprinted on a rare wet day, materializes now and again coming up, but we lose them on the rimrock. Most afternoons, wind sweeps the sandy wash above the pourover clean, and in the next half mile the only human sign is a few juniper logs cleverly arranged into a waist-high conical structure. Another half mile brings a handful of pot sherds, strewn among a few rusted tin cans. Two or three well-placed rock piles mark a route into the next canyon.

A splash of bright orange on a little dune draws me like a magnet. A cooler? A life jacket? Ah, a plastic road cone, God knows how many desert

*All day long
 may I walk.
Through the
 returning seasons
 may I walk.
On the trail marked
 with pollen
 may I walk.
With grasshoppers
 about my feet
 may I walk.
With dew
 about my feet
 may I walk.
With beauty
 may I walk.*

*The Night Chant,
The Second Day*

miles from the nearest road. The latest in cairns? Not litter up here but an enigma, a story I can't crack. On the other hand, our own swath of footprints down on the adobe trail leaves little to the imagination. Lake boaters. At what point, I wonder, do traces become impact.

Back at the top of the Wingate, we sprawl on the slickrock rim, reluctant to leave Earth Woman's domain. From here we can revel in the far view. Mountains float above pale waves of sandstone, Natsis'áán just yonder, and to the north and east the "blue mystery" of the Henrys. Almost straight down, the only dissonance; water gleaming like a fallen piece of sky.

# Sleeping Out

EARTH WOMAN'S CHINLE skirts are dragging in the lake. The shales are rumpled and faded in the afternoon sun, gray muslins streaked with burnt orange, as if she had been gathering clay on the muddy bank when the flood came. The dark blue water, pooled at her thighs and moving only with the wind, astonishes a mind evolved in nature. All that broken country ending abruptly at this machine-polished edge.

Camp is a ratty bit of mauve clay, littered with tamarisk and hunks of driftwood swirled down the mountain on summer floods. An unwalkable morass of mud and sticks clogs the mouth of the creek. My bed, perched on a fold in the skirt, is an old aluminum cot lugged up to span the rocks and wrinkles. Above my head, on the mountain and her mesas, life prowls and whispers and scavenges all night long. At my feet only the occasional fish, jumping into a broth of stars and falling back, breaks the quiet.

Topographic logic—along with the surprises which overlay order like coyote's leftover stars tossed across the constellations—is smoothed over. Water, dead water, hushes the buzz and hum of living and dying. On the reservoir, the grand changes of fall into winter, night into day wheel along, but the smaller turnings, the interlocking gears of creation, seem lost and gone.

I play at imagining a meteor plunging into the shimmering mirror, sending waves of water to topple the dam. Slightly more likely is the removal of the dam by an enlightened body politic. Maybe my best bet is mud, acres of mud, clogging the turbines; or a spate of hundred year floods.

Eric teased on and on last spring about the bilagáana obsession with clocks and daybooks. In this immensity of desert and sky, historical time feels trivial, even irrelevant. No matter the scenario

*Morning, Again*

*Shadow-floating*
*on my silver cot*
*my pillow doubled*
*under my head*

*I am pulled*
*from sleep by*
*the whip-whip*
*of raven wings*

*An orange flash*
*and the cliffs*
*pulsate*
*coals fanned*

*to life*
*in the half*
*light of a*
*newborn dawn*

*embers slumping*
*into stained*
*and melted*
*glass*

*Raven-drawn*
*the glossy wind*
*blows new life*
*into the whorls*

*on my scalp*
*my fingertips*
*The fiery water*
*crumples*

*corrugated here*
*with black*
*and to the west*
*with azure*

*Ann Weiler Walka*

of its demise, the monolithic Glen Canyon Dam stands as impermanent as the old ones' check-dams on the dry washes.

I'm utterly content on my silver cot. A pillow from home under my head, my old Pendleton blanket pulled over my sleeping bag—there are some great things about traveling by houseboat—I ruminate about Earth Woman's neighborhood. Of all the places I camp out, this feels like the most lived-in by humans, and also the wildest.

Tomorrow we should talk about belonging to a place without undoing it. Especially when it's too late to be sparse. Walk lots. Keep your mind here and now. Widen your peripheral vision (Eli, an intern, taught me that just yesterday). Learn to garden without hoses. Savor the task, everyday, of participating in creation. Watch out for your neighbors, no matter their phylum. Keep it simple. Like your mother always said, be appropriate. Walk some more.

# Sleeping on the Lap of Earth Woman

My silver cot perched on a sandstone knoll
is a pedestal on a pedestal. I ache
to be gathered up by dark arms
and lifted into sky.

Plains people know the real world
arches over our heads, its songlines
mapped by the constellations.
Earth is ephemeral, a moon on a lake.

Tonight catfish leap
for barbs of light, gleaming,
splashing and slipping back,
swaying dreamrocked in black silk.

In my sleep I sink and shoot upward,
arcing through stars, a meteor,
sparking, freefalling,
flaring again.


Bald Rock

# Lullaby

Tamarisk feathering
pale sand
Water lapping

Like the wavelets
I rise and fall
in and out of dreaming

All day I walked
Stone sparkled underfoot
dissolving into sand

And light   light
pinyon jays laughing
at the wisp of a moon

A Basketmaker camp
slabs folded into burned earth
bright blue sky

I am rising and falling
in and out of sleep
hard body to breath body

Smiling at the fleece
stretched dappled across
the face of the moon

Wind brushes my face
I lift my cheek
floating up from a dream

Something lovely
sails past the moon
spirits traveling by water

The river oh the lake
I dreamed you rustle
and murmur over stones

Rays of dark
fan from the lake
stream into sky


The San Juan Arm

Scorpion Gulch

Harris Wash

Henry Mountains

Dirty Devil River

Escalante (Unknown) River

Waterpocket Fold

Coyote Gulch

Forty Mile Ridge

Straight Cliffs

Glen Canyon of the Colorado River

Dance Hall Rock
X

Davis Gulch
X

Hole-in-the-Rock

Kaiparowits Plateau

San Juan River

Paria River

Rainbow Plateau

Navajo Mountain

Flagstaff

Naatsis' áán

Home

# Coming Home

April, 1991, my fiftieth-birthday trip, and the wind gusts dark and raw. We bounced down the old wagon road to this alcove sculpted from a dome of Entrada sandstone, talking about the Mormon Hole-in-the-Rock expedition. Now a few of us—on the first day of our trip, most folks are shy—bow to imaginary partners and waltz double-time across a sandrock floor. It was a long drive today, across the Colorado and up along the Paria, through the Blue Hills to the tiny town of Escalante and then forty miles back south on the dirt road beneath the Straight Cliffs. I had to ride in the bouncy back seat. With outstretched arms, I spin until I'm dizzy.

When the wagon train gathered in November of 1879, Dance Hall Rock was the end of the road. Answering a call from the Mormon church, over 200 Saints with 80 wagons and nearly a thousand head of livestock scattered their camps near here, 25 miles short of the rim of Glen Canyon and just west of the canyon of the Escalante. On their way to secure the southeast corner of Deseret from the forces of disorder—Texas cattlemen, outlaws, and Indians—families clustered around Forty-Mile Spring for three wintry weeks. There were fiddles in the party, and scuffed boots tapped and skirts swung when they danced in the Hall "where nature had made the smooth flat rock floor on purpose."

The accounts when they came were sobering. Platte Lyman, their erstwhile leader, warned that "the country here is almost entirely sand rock, high hills and mountains cut all to pieces by deep gulches which are in many places altogether impassable. It is certainly the worst country I ever saw." He continued that "most of us are satisfied that there is no use of this company undertaking to get through to San Juan this way." They did,

*How they ever found their way through deep snow and blinding snow storms in such a broken timbered country, all cut to pieces with deep gorges, for such a long distance, without compass, trail, and most of the time no sun, moon, or stars to help them in keeping their course is a mystery. The only answer is that a kind Providence came to their assistance in answer to their humble fervent prayers...Their experience almost made the journey of the good Catholic Escalante look like a picnic party.*

*Kumen Jones*

though, snow blocking their retreat, and momen-
tum and faith being what they are.

The men of the expedition spent six weeks blasting and shoring up the Hole-in-the-Rock, a wagon
road descending 1800 feet down a nearly vertical
crack to the Colorado River. The women set up
housekeeping on the blackbrush flats above the
canyons. Young Lizzie Decker assured her parents
that her boys "Genie and Willie are as fat as little
pigs and just as full of fun as they can be... Genie
has just been playing horse out to the woodpile
[and] Willie is out there with Rowly's Children
making a dugway and playing he is blasting the
Hole in the Rock down. We have got the stove in
the wagon and it is quite comfortable."

On January 26 the pioneers worked the wagons
down the Hole and across the river ("It nearly scared
me to death," Lizzie wrote). It took until April to
make another hundred miles or so to a cottonwood-
shaded bottom on the San Juan. A few weeks later,
Lizzie complained "I have been takeing bitters for a
week but Ive been telling Em that I guess it is the
effects of liveing out in the cold all winter, now liveing out in the heat through the summer and its just
thawing the frozen bread out that we eat last winter
and no wonder we feel a fool. I am going to have a
house this week and then it will take four yoke of
oxen to ever get me out of it again."

INSTEAD OF following the old Mormon road, we
turn east this evening and rattle over a rutted two-
track to the head of a trail down to the Unknown
River. The wind is screaming. We set up a table in
the lee of the van and try to make dinner while
occasional gusts blow the pots off the table. Soon
enough, though, Don's Moroccan stew and a spark-
showering fire, not to mention birthday champagne,
make us "quite comfortable."

*You want us to tell you
what kind of a country
this is but I don't know
how. It's the roughest
country you or anybody
else ever seen; it's nothing in the world but
rocks and holes, hills
and hollows. The moun-
tains are just one solid
rock as smooth as an
apple.*

*Lizzie Decker*

## Dance Hall Rock

A gray wind scours the hollowed stone
spitting snow in our faces,
sawing like a bow.

>Dance in a hollow
>in a snow-glinting sandstorm;
>a fiddle tune howling in the swirling wind.

A girl, laughing,
stamps her heels
on slickrock,
her skirt twirling
around her boot tops,
chapped hands clapping
over her head.

>Dance like the wind
>spinning through sagebrush,
>twist like the junipers tossing on the rim.

She hates the house promised
at the trek's end,
sandstone blocks
quarried straight
as rules and mortared
into snugness.

>Dance with your tongue
>out, capturing snowflakes;
>dance with your fingertips weaving into wind.

She hates the husband
yet unchosen
who builds
the house.

She hates the parlor,
yet unplanned
where she spends
her evenings knitting.
She hates the children
yet undreamed
who come down smelling of soap
to kiss her good night.

      Waltz into a canyon,
      a dark flowing canyon,
      dance into the shadow and drift and spin.

She loves wind tugging at her hair
and the sage-stippled sandflat
flowing without fences
to the red breaks.
She loves no furniture to dust or lace to sew
and stars as dense
as snowflakes in a blizzard.
She loves a fiddle tune
soaring on a storm.

      Dance with the boy
      you kissed behind a wagon,
      dance with his hand on your warm white skin.

Pray gentle parents,
you get her to a town
before it's too late.


Dance Hall Rock

THE NEXT MORNING we divvy up the food and group gear—please, won't someone take this last fuel bottle—fuss with the load, and, wincing, hoist our packs. Gathering up above the Crack-in-the-Wall, a route through the sheer sandstone wall down to the Unknown River, we marvel at the scene to the east. Across the canyons of the Escalante, beyond the Circle Cliffs and the Waterpocket Fold, the Henry Mountains, Thompson's clue to the wrong river, lift like an August cloud bank.

EVERETT RUESS'S LAST letter home was headed Escalante Rim, Utah, November 11 (1934). Four years before, when he was sixteen, Everett left his genteelly bohemian family home in Los Angeles to hitchhike into Navajo territory beyond the Colorado. Brimming with innocence and nerve, he fashioned for himself the life of a "vagabond for beauty," picking up odd jobs here and there or even better, finding supper and shelter with generous strangers. Mostly he wandered the formidable country with his string of burros (he named one Everett to remind himself what he used to be), drawing and recounting his saga in letters home, avid for any experience which would enmesh him in his new god, beauty. He wrote with disdain of his fellow Anglos (largely traders, including the likes of John Wetherill) "that they are deaf, dumb and blind to it all… They think of nothing but money." Three years into his ecstatic's quest, Ruess jotted in his diary his two rules for life—"…never count the cost, and never do anything unless you can do it whole heartedly. Now is the time to live."

A few months later he appeared in Escalante where he "stopped a few days and indulged myself in family life…If I had stayed any longer I would have fallen in love with a Mormon girl." Eager instead for the bliss of undomesticated country, he headed

*My camp is on the very point of the divide, with the country falling away to the blue horizon on the east and west. Northward is the sheer face of Mount Kaiparowitz, pale vermillion capped with white, a forested summit. West and south are desert and distant mountains. Tonight the pale crescent of the new moon appeared for a little while, low on the skyline, at sunset. Often as I wander, there are dream-like tinges when life seems impossibly strange and unreal…*

*Everett Ruess*

toward the Hole-in-the-Rock with his little pack train. From camp at the edge of town, he wrote to his brother, Waldo, that "a few days ago I rode into the red rocks and sandy desert again, and it was like coming home." Except for the pseudonym "NEMO" and "1934", carved near a ruin in Davis Gulch, some fifty miles south of town, Everett was never seen or heard from again.

Largely through his letters and woodcuts, Everett became a culture hero for backpacking pilgrims. I told his story to my new friends last night, and the youngster's light-mindedness accompanies us this morning as we descend behind the spalled-off slab and across the leaning dune toward the confluence of Coyote Gulch and the Escalante. We're about to make a thirty-some-mile circle up the Gulch, across Kings Mesa, and back down the river.

THE SWEEP AGAIN, I trail the ragged procession into a side canyon hung with black silk and limey seeps. Green light filters from cottonwoods and pale-fingered oaks. Heading upstream we turn a bend guarded by buffalo warriors, mudded high above our head centuries ago by some Fremont visionary and protected all these years by an overhang.

Single file, we follow Don out of the creekbed and into a dark, insistent wind. Tired of tagging along, I drop farther behind the little line, content to find my own way up between the mounds of slickrock and ebony pools. There's scant soil to take a footprint here, and despite my independent spirit, I'm pleased when I spot my companions hunkered out of the weather, packs resting on a shelf of rock.

Today is my very birthday. We camp in a white-slipped slickrock bowl just below a divide. Despite the gray chill, sand pockets flower with tiny tequilia and evening primrose. A lovely young woman struggles to pitch her blue and yellow tent in the badgering wind.

*As to when I shall visit civilization, it will not be soon, I think. I have not tired of the wilderness; rather I enjoy its beauty and the vagrant life I lead, more keenly all the time... Do you blame me then for staying here, where I feel that I belong and am one with the world around me?*

*Everett Ruess*

Why fight this gale? I slip off into the lee of a sandstone knob and watch the moon float up like a bubble from a sea of rose-tinted shadow. Navajo Mountain, Earth Woman, blushing under her veil of clouds, inclines her head. I bow in return. We three, me, the moon, the mountain; our dark innards are belied by faces reflecting the sun.

Coming down in the rain from Kings Divide, we make the scary friction-climb and beat a path through the beaver works. Today my trajectory, buoyant sometimes as the moon, is deformed by gravity. At the end of a long trudge, we sleep deep in the interior of the country.

USUALLY I STROLL the Escalante country as blissful as young Mr. Ruess, but this time I'm unsettled, my own strata worn through by walking. On my pilgrimage, down, up, over, and down, I study on merging two lives, one as wild and free as Everett's and the lovely young woman's, the other dense with obligation and affection, not to mention expectation. Lagging past the pools that first day, I encountered bedrock—my childhood summers on the granite shores of a Canadian lake, stomping off alone with my fishing pole. When my own kids grew up, weary of being the household mainstay, I gloried in splitting myself between that feral child and a sometime grownup. Now I am eager to braid the two strands back together. Take the outback to town, bring my other life here.

Two days downstream, we rise early, heading for home. The river—warmer on this brilliant blue morning—makes perfect wading, and I'm getting to know her conformation, her deeps and shallows, the shape of her sandbars. Chuckling, she smooths my scratched legs; her cool weight parts around me, flows through me. Humming to ourselves, the lovely young woman and I go down together.

# Climbing at Night at Scorpion Butte

Surely I dreamed myself into this world
where stone hills gleam like upturned
bowls. Climbing I press my palms
on dented pewter, wedge bare
feet into shadow.

There is a pool curved into a crevice
between the hills, a sliver
of white shell shimmering
on its sleek black skin.

The moon sighs as delicately
as a petal falling on yellow grass,
a cloud passing.

A man I knew claimed he carried the moon
in his pocket. I see now
she is her own person.

Blowing away the dust I drink her light
which keeps wrinkling
on the water.


Scorpion Butte

# Local Knowledge

*Paths to the world of dawn,*
*of evening, and of darkness*
*pass through the pole star,*
*the axis of the world.*

Chuckchi

Slip into a canyon choked with tamarisk
and deerflies; skirt the quicksand
left by the spring floods; ford
the muddy creek.
              Stop at the first fork,
two cracks twisting into red sandstone;
no hints given.
              Sit with your back
against a rock, seining
the downcanyon winds for feathers,
pollen drifting, the breath
of foxes.
            When your water is gone
choose a way.  Past the narrows
musky with monkey flowers
a pool trembles
beneath a spring.
There will be frogs bawling now
and a tumble of wren song.

This may be an anteroom to heaven
but there is no way up.
When darkness settles onto your
shoulders like doubt,
backtrack.

A slickrock cliff slopes into sky.
You must find your way by touch,
feeling for a feasible pitch,
toeholds, the cold prick
of stars.
          Lie on your back
in a swale filled with sand;
wait for the handle to nick
your palm.
                From here you know
how to find the pole star.


A Canyon on the Lower Escalante

# Harris Wash

THE TERRAIN Everett Ruess admired from Navajo Mountain "as... impenetrable a territory as I have ever seen..." has come in the years since my fiftieth birthday to signify the realm where poems are born. I'm pleased to be here on another April morning—having walked from bare-branched winter into spring—with a group of women who want to explore both without and within. With my friend Ellen Meloy, I am leading a writing/hiking workshop deep in the landscape of my imagination.

On the floor of Harris Wash, swinging around the great bends, wading the ankle-deep creek, the "impenetrable territory" becomes intimate and comforting. The women, most of them first-time backpackers, seem to be trusting it too. We walk one by one down the creek to the Escalante, each of us stopping along the way to imagine a story which illuminates the character of a stretch of the canyon.

Just downstream of the last woman's chosen spot, I drop happily onto damp sand, my feet, planted on the smooth bed, minor obstructions in the stream that spills around them. While I daydream, the creek quickens, a train of miniature haystacks billowing past my ankles for a moment or two. Languishing fast, the waves slacken underfoot, first to a corrugated V and then to a brilliant slick, and the creek basks again. Why does the water surge suddenly and then subside?

Tracy splashes by me, her songline stanza written on the back of her hand. I jot down a story for this Bend Where Water Hurries Down. The little black phoebe wavering on the willow branch just upstream plays the *mayordomo* here. When she flies up to feast on a swarm of midges, the water swings after her, and as she swoops above her familiar stretch of wrinkling light, she tugs the wavelets along. Perching again, the diminutive homebody's swell of excitement flows on down, fattening the stream like a frog squeezed through a garter snake's belly. Why not? Everything is connected to everything.

On our last morning in a new-green cottonwood bosque, nurtured by this play, this place, we contemplate returning to our other lives. I read a Navajo prayer for homecoming.

> ...Beautifully my country to me
>       is restored
> Beautifully my fields to me
>       are restored
> Beautifully my house to me
>       is restored...

FOR MOST OF US home is taking care; comforting associations of belongings; familiar landscapes embroidered with custom and story. Again and again on this hike, stories from here evoked stories from there. The time away rooted the women more deeply in Vermont and Ontario and Montana, farflung places which support and count on them. They liked walking the Unknown River but, like Lizzie Decker, they are ready to be in a house again.

Two or three felt deeply comfortable and comforted in this canyon, felt at home, as Everett did, as we do in particular places, even strange ones. Entirely present, they embraced Lopez's "gifts of eye and ear, of tongue and nose and finger." Maybe an unexpected sympathy for invertebrates was born. Or a new quiet, or a delicacy of step. Perhaps Harris Wash will haunt the imagination and flower again in a journal, a hummed melody, a poem jotted on a grocery list. Another stanza in the songline that laces us to our continent.

*Through the middle
of broad fields
the rainbow
returned with me
To where my house
is visible
the rainbow
returned with me
To the entrance
of my house
the rainbow
returned with me
To just within
my house
the rainbow
returned with me
To my fireside
the rainbow
returned with me*

*The Night Chant,
The Second Day*

# Finding the Patterns: The Poet as Scientist

I'm sweeping around the bends of the canyon
like a raven banking from wall

                     to wall, merging with his shadow,
wheeling away;

like the ten-year-old I used to be, slaloming
down a brick street on a fat-tired bike,

                             pigtails flying.

A forty-pound pack dampens my speed but I still feel
the sine waves flow through
the soles of my boots.
                   Bend after bend after
bend, points of inflection swing me
and the knee-deep, gleaming river
                         headlong into
rushes of light, lapis-shadowed eddies.

I am a pendulum describing an arc of river,
a curve of sandstone.

                We are simply ordered. The river and the sheer
                   fall of cliffs. Me and the raven, cawing,
                     and a beaver I saw waddling at sunrise

                   down a light-flecked gravel bar. Two equal
surfaces and three transitively connected objects.
                 Simply ordered; although our pattern

                   is obscured by the delicate track of a fox
                         circling around willows.

Simple motion; wading downstream, spiraling into
        the other world through a helix
            of water-swirled rock.
                                Morning,
                    uncoiling from alcoves,
            from the channel hollowed by
a milky river, illuminates the spin,
the spaces.

            Air simmering like honey. Green-splitting
                    slivers of light. Shadow flowing.
We are all whirlwinds unwinding.


The Escalante

## The Mayfly

A nymph
clasped by
the silken fist
of water, I slipped
from instar to instar, feasting
in the dark on sweet red
mud, the delicate
piquance of algae,
my belly heavy
and satisfied.
               Now I float
on sheer dusk; no belly at all;
twilight shining
inside me.

Imagoes,
imagined ones,
we seethed into brilliant ether,
leaving our souls
to drift on the river's
skin.

          No histories, no dreams.
We are burning alive,
a company of ecstatics,
a column of desire.


Escalante River

# Coming Home

ALTHOUGH I ONLY pass through here now and
again, Earth Woman's field of view lies at the dead
center of my imagination. And like Everett, when I
am here I feel like I belong to the place.

I don't stay for long though. I'm 58, not 18.
Once I daydreamed about trading in my life on
Cherry Street to chase butterflies or spotted owls,
to start a field school or squat in some redrock
canyon. Now I'm a matriarch, thriving on gardens
and granddaughters, on coffee in bed and cooking
indoors out of the wind, on making poems with
kids about places they love. My moveable life is
happily centered in my hometown.

And my visits are simply that. I've never gar-
dened here, at the head of some mostly dry wash,
or even on Potato Valley's ditch system. I haven't
tried to make a bird snare with my own hair or to
find a cow in a sandstone maze.

On the other hand, I won't be a tourist in my
heart's terrain. Guiding, even though I plan fewer
trips each year, means I work here. In Naatsis'áán's
purview, as well as in the pine woods at the end of
my street, I know the flowers, the birds, the local
gossip. I'm familiar with the habits of water, the
casts of light. Comfortable sleeping on the ground.
As vigilant in defense of community as an absent-
minded itinerant can be.

MUSING ON HOME, I reflect on what that meant to
the characters wandering in and out of this book.
The Archaic people and the Paiutes, the hunters
and gatherers, must have felt at home not simply in
a particular canyon but in the sweep of space that
they covered in their seasonal rounds. The Navajos
who came seeking refuge, discovered Diné Tah,
homeland, waiting when they arrived.

Only a few Anglos ever settled deep enough—
like John and Louisa Wetherill—to learn language,

landscape and local custom. Everett vowed to stay, but, like many an ardent lover, burned too bright to endure. Lizzie made her family "at home" for a while above the Hole-in-the-Rock, but had no doubt that the real thing was back there and up ahead, a town, a house.

Powell and his Survey crew showed up for eight years of field seasons. I'm curious whether John Wesley carried the landscape in his heart when his own field work here tapered to nothing. As Director of the United States Geologic Survey and Director of the Bureau of Ethnology at the Smithsonian, the people and landscapes of this dry country remained the focus of his prodigious work in Washington D.C., though from 1880 to his death in Maine in 1902, he scarcely returned to the Colorado River country.

IN BETWEEN my own field seasons, the Glen Canyon Basin stretches out there empty and vibrantly alive. From time to time when my hometown web pulls too tight, I imagine a particular cranny humming along without me, lovely and indifferent under its weathering sky, and I am steadied and soothed.

Somehow this place, above all the others I love and despite her vast scar, has become solace, ballast, refuge, the far end of my home range.

More dreamed, perhaps, than accurately remembered—like those vivid and entirely personal childhood memories no one else can summon up—the terrain has marked me.

There are tangible benefits to being marked by wilderness. I see it in my guiding friends. A wild heart could care less about owning it all. The empty spaces we carry in our belly invite us to live within whispering distance of our neighbors, to savor closeness, to think small. Earth Woman's energy sparkling in our veins goads us into artful lives. The wind tracks on our skin make us grateful for a shower, for shelter.

And time Out There leaves us with a changed notion of the scale of things. Under Earth Woman's gaze, in real life or in memory, dailiness loses its grip on my imagination. I realize both my insignificance—ah, light-mindedness—and the archetypal elements of my own story.

I don't live in her unfathomable landscape, but the country lives in me. I would be lost without it.

Such is the American reliance on wilderness. Surely John Wesley, harassed and finally deeply hurt by political adversaries in Washington, turned his mind back toward the Great Unknown. Drifted again on the muddy river slipping through his veins.

*It is finished in beauty.*
*In the house of evening light.*
*From the story made of evening light.*
*On the trail of evening light.*
*O, House God!*

*Traditional Navajo song*

## Flow Report

My life runs through me like a river.

In November the pools turn over,
deep shadows surfacing,
my own light sinking to the bottom.

All winter I run as slow and quiet
as barely melted bronze.
Sometimes ice floes raft on my back and twist
down the current, flashing at the sky.
These reflections have nothing
to do with my secret life.

In the spring I overflow my banks and spread myself
as far as I can,
moving quickly and laughing often.

This summer evening I am rich with mud and
leaves and fish arcing through the dusk
and swallows dipping into my dreams.

Season after season, I go on down,
rushing along, circling back,
braiding and meandering,
gathering in and letting go,
deepening, opening,
intent on the sea.


Home

# Sources of Quotations

Beautiful House Song. Translated in Cosmos Mindeleff's "Navajo Houses" (1898)

Lizzie Decker. Letters from David E. Miller's *Hole in the Rock* (1959)

Frederick Dellenbaugh. *A Canyon Voyage* (1908)

Clarence Dutton. *Geology of the High Plateaus* (1880)

Fr. Silvestre Velez de Escalante. Journal excerpts from Warner's *The Dominguez-Escalante Journal* (1995)

Kumen Jones. A recollection from David E. Miller's *Hole in the Rock* (1959)

Ellsworth Kolb. *Through the Grand Canyon from Wyoming to Mexico* (1914)

Clyde Kluckhohn. *To the Foot of the Rainbow* (1927)

Katie Lee. *All My Rivers Are Gone* (1998)

Barry Lopez. "American Geographies" *About This Life: Journeys on the Threshhold of Memory* (1998)

CM, a Navajo Singer named only by his initials. From James McNeley's *Holy Wind in Navajo Philosophy* (1981)

Ernest Nelson, a Navajo Singer. From Karl Luckert's *Navajo Mountain and Rainbow Bridge Religion* (1977)

Night Chant, Ninth Day. Lines from the ninth day of the Navajo Night Chant as translated in Larry Fagin's *The List Poem* (1991)

Night Chant, Second Day. Lines from the second day of the Navajo Night Chant. Translated by Washington Matthews in *Navajo Myths, Prayers and Songs* (in the University of California Publications in American Archeology and Ethnology, 5:2) (1907)

Paiute Story. Collected by Powell and printed in Fowler and Euler's *John Wesley Powell and the Anthropology of the Canyon Country* (1969)

John Wesley Powell. *The Exploration of the Colorado River and its Canyons* (First printed in 1895 as *Canyons of the Colorado*)

Everett Ruess. From W. L. Rusho's *Everett Ruess: A Vagabond for Beauty* (1983)

Slim Woman. From Karl Luckert's *Navajo Mountain and Rainbow Bridge Religion* (1977)

Almon Thompson. From Powell's *Exploration of the Colorado River of the West and its Tributaries* (1875)

# References

Abbey, Edward. 1968. *Desert Solitaire: A Season in the Wilderness* (New York: McGraw Hill)

Crampton, Gregory. 1988. *The Ghosts of Glen Canyon: History Beneath Lake Powell* (St. George, Utah: Publishers Place, Inc.)

Dellenbaugh, Frederick. 1908. *A Canyon Voyage* (New York: G.P. Putnam's Sons)

Dutton, Clarence. 1880. *Geology of the High Plateaus* (Washington D.C.: Government Printing Office)

Fagin, Larry. 1991. *The List Poem* (New York: Teachers and Writers Collaborative)

Fowler, Don D., Robert C. Euler, and Catherine S. Fowler. 1969. *John Wesley Powell and the Anthropology of the Canyon Country, Geological Survey Professional Paper* 670 (Washington, D. C.: Government Printing Office)

Geary, Edward A. 1992. *The Proper Edge of Sky: The High Plateau Country of Utah* (Salt Lake City, Utah: University of Utah Press)

Jennings, Jesse D. 1966. *Glen Canyon: A Summary*, University of Utah Anthropological Paper No. 81 (Salt Lake City, Utah: University of Utah Press)

Kluckhohn, Clyde. 1927. *To the Foot of the Rainbow* (New York: Century)

Kolb, Ellsworth. 1914. *Through the Grand Canyon from Wyoming to Mexico* (New York: MacMillan)

Lambrechtse, Rudi. 1985. *Hiking the Escalante* (Salt Lake City, Utah: Wasatch Publishers, Inc.)

Lee, Katie. 1998. *All My Rivers Are Gone* (Boulder, Colorado: Johnson Books)

Lopez, Barry. 1998. "American Geographies" in *About This Life: Journeys on the Threshhold of Memory* (New York, NY: Alfred A Knopf)

Luckert, Karl. 1977. *Navajo Mountain and Rainbow Bridge Religion* (Flagstaff, Arizona: Museum of Northern Arizona)

Matthews, Washington and P. E. Goddard, editor. 1907. *Navajo Myths, Prayers, and Songs*, University of California Publications in American Archeololgy and Ethnology, 5:2 (Berkeley, California: The University Press)

McNeley, James K. 1981. *Holy Wind in Navajo Philosophy* (Tucson, Arizona: University of Arizona Press)

McPherson, Robert S. 1992. *Sacred Land, Sacred View: Navajo Perceptions of the Four Corners Region*, Charles Redd Monographs in Western History No. 19 (Provo, Utah: Brigham Young University)

Miller, David E. 1959. *Hole in the Rock* (Salt Lake City, Utah: University of Utah Press)

Mindeleff, Cosmos. 1898. "Navajo Houses" in Smithsonian Institution: *Bureau of American Ethnology Annual Report* 17 (Washington D.C.: Government Printing Office)

Porter, Elliot. 1963. *The Place No One Knew: Glen Canyon of the Colorado* (Salt Lake City, Utah: Peregrine Smith Books)

Powell, John Wesley. 1875. *Exploration of the Colorado River of the West and it's Tributaries* (Washington D.C.: Government Printing Office)

_____. 1895. *Canyons of the Colorado* (Reprinted in 1961 as *The Exploration of the Colorado River and its Canyons* (New York: Dover Publications, Inc.)

Rusho, W. L. 1983. *Everett Ruess: A Vagabond for Beauty* (Salt Lake City, Utah: Peregrine Smith Books)

Stegner, Wallace. 1954. *Beyond the Hundredth Meridian: John Wesley Powell and the Second Opening of the West* (Boston: Houghton Mifflin)

Topping, Gary. 1997. *Glen Canyon and the San Juan Country* (Moscow, Idaho: University of Idaho Press)

Walka, Ann Weiler. 1994. "Lake Powell: A Canyon Transformed", *Plateau* Vol. 65:2 (Flagstaff, Arizona: Museum of Northern Arizona)

Warner, Ted J., editor. 1995. *The Dominguez-Escalante Journal: The Expedition Through Colorado, Utah, Arizona and New Mexico in 1776* (Salt Lake City, Utah: The University of Utah Press)

## About the Author

A poet and naturalist and a stubborn generalist, Ann trains her curiosity and imagination on a landscape's weave of geologic processes, life stories, ecological relationships—all the pattern and surprise which make up the world. In writing down the tapestry, she engages more fully with the terrain.

Ann came to the southwest 35 years ago and fell in love with the desert while she tended her kids and studied renewable resource management at the University of Arizona. A career in museum education brought her to the Museum of Northern Arizona (MNA), an institution which aims to explore and explain the Colorado Plateau. For fifteen years she has led expeditions into the Plateau backcountry for MNA and other field institutes.

Pieces from Ann's first book, *Waterlines: Journeys on a Desert River*, a collection of poems and stories inspired by the San Juan River earned a Fellowship from the Arizona Commission on the Arts. A chapbook of poems about the Escalante and Glen Canyon, *Walking the Unknown River: Travels in the Heart of a Far Country*, accompanied an exhibit at MNA which featured the writing. Her poems and essays are published in literary and environmental journals—*Plateau Journal*, *Petroglyph*, and *Borderlands* are a few—on gallery walls and, best of all, are read aloud in the outback.